OWN YOUR CAREER

OWN
YOUR
CAREER

MICHELA ALLOCCA

OWN YOUR CAREER

BREAK THE CORPORATE BLUEPRINT & BUILD YOUR OWN LADDER

WILEY

Published by John Wiley & Sons, Inc., Hoboken, New Jersey.
Published simultaneously in Canada.

For general information on our other products and services or for technical support, please contact our Customer Care Department within the United States at (800) 762-2974, outside the United States at (317) 572-3993 or fax (317) 572-4002.

Wiley also publishes its books in a variety of electronic formats. Some content that appears in print may not be available in electronic formats. For more information about Wiley products, visit our web site at www.wiley.com.

Library of Congress Cataloging-in-Publication Data

Names: Allocca, Michela, author.
Title: Own your career : break the corporate blueprint and build your own
  ladder / Michela Allocca.
Description: Hoboken, New Jersey : Wiley, [2024] | Includes index.
Identifiers: LCCN 2024006656 (print) | LCCN 2024006657 (ebook) | ISBN
  9781394195275 (cloth) | ISBN 9781394195299 (adobe pdf) | ISBN
  9781394195282 (epub)
Subjects: LCSH: Career development. | Vocational guidance. | Success in
  business.
Classification: LCC HF5381 .A64 2024 (print) | LCC HF5381 (ebook) | DDC
  650.1—dc23/eng/20240322
LC record available at https://lccn.loc.gov/2024006656
LC ebook record available at https://lccn.loc.gov/2024006657

Cover Design: Wiley
Cover Image : © Elena Emchuk /Shutterstock, © Munerf.std/Shutterstock
Author Photo: Courtesy of the Author
SKY10074691_050924

Contents

Acknowledgments

Writing a book will always be a humbling experience, and I am truly grateful to have been given the opportunity to write not just one, but two books in my 20s. I'd first like to thank my entire family for their unconditional support on my entrepreneurial journey. I would also like to share my appreciation for the wonderful publishing team at Wiley, who has provided extensive support and guidance to bring this book to life. And finally, I want to thank the entire Break Your Budget community for believing in me, following me, and allowing me to pursue my dreams in ways I could have never imagined. We are just getting started!

Introduction

Most college graduates enter corporate America because they've been told that this is the path to long-term happiness and success. It's never questioned or challenged, and usually after a few months or maybe a year, they realize this:

Everything you've been told about working? *It's a lie.*

Your dream job? *It's an illusion.*

Climbing the corporate ladder to become a CEO? *It's unlikely.*

At least for the majority of people. According to the Bureau of Labor Statistics (BLS 2023b), in 2022 there were an estimated 199,240 "chief executives" in the labor market. For context, the 2022 labor market was estimated to include approximately 164 million people (BLS 2023a). That means that—generously—0.1% of workers will reach the C-suite.

Sure, that could be you—but it probably won't be. And that's okay!

It's normal to enter the workforce feeling motivated, excited, and ready to conquer the world. I hate to be the bearer of bad news, but that feeling is fleeting, and if you want to find true happiness at work, you'll need to define it on your own terms. I know it sounds scary and depressing, but that's what I'm here for.

It's become far too commonplace to find yourself 15 years deep into a career that is wholly unsatisfying, and to feel absolutely lost on how to find purpose at work. The reality of spending the majority of your life working is overwhelming.

It doesn't have to be that way.

Who Do I Think I Am, Anyway?

Whether you picked up this book after following me on social media for a while, or if you are brand-new to my story—you might be wondering who do I think I am to tell you that you're probably not going to hit that C-suite?

Let me fill you in, because there was a time when I thought that the college-to-corporate CEO path was the only one that would result in success.

I graduated college bright-eyed and bushy-tailed with a corporate job lined up. You'll hear all the details in subsequent chapters, but here's the TL;DR: working was not all it's cracked up to be.

I always thought that when I graduated college and landed that "dream job," I'd be all set. Over time I would get promoted, I'd easily start making more money, and I'd become this boss powerhouse who ran meetings and was important. Maybe I was unusually naive, but I think I was just inexperienced. You don't know what you don't know!

What I learned the hard way is that not only is this reality not common, but I didn't want it. I didn't know *what* I wanted, because honestly, I never really thought about what I would do beyond that first job. I figured it would all just fall into place over time. I spent my whole life up to that point preparing to get the job, and once I was in it without a clear path laid out in front of me anymore, I freaked out.

This experience isn't unique, but how I decided to navigate it is. About two years after I started my first job, I was on the phone with my best friend Emily, who had recently left her teaching job to pursue her own health-coaching business full-time. She was asking me questions about personal finance and made the suggestion that I consider starting my own social media page sharing all the tips and advice I was giving to her. This was the beginning of a new chapter of my life that I didn't even realize would change everything for me. After that conversation, I created a new Instagram handle called *Break Your Budget*, and the rest is history.

You'll hear more about this journey in Chapter 7, but starting this endeavor served as an outlet for me. I wasn't happy at work, I had free time outside of my nine-to-five, and I was looking for more. Since work wasn't giving me *more*, I created it myself.

I shared lessons I learned on the job, leveraged skills I already had to create digital products, began working with clients to help them budget better, and consistently posted on social media. It was the perfect combination of fueling my creativity outside of the office and helping people with a skill I was already passionate about.

Most importantly, it helped me find clarity on what I wanted out of my career and how I could find my own definition of success. I had spent so much time pursuing society's definition of success and completely ignoring what could actually make me happy.

I hated client service at work, but I loved working with clients via Break Your Budget. I hated working in Excel at the office, but I loved leveraging it to create budgeting templates. I never had the opportunity at work to be creative or to use social media, but I loved posting on Instagram and sharing lessons with my followers.

It was through Break Your Budget that I discovered that there may be more to finding happiness through work than I initially thought. I learned that there *are* ways to marry making money with pursuing something you actually enjoy. And most importantly, I discovered that what I deem a successful career path for *myself* may look different than what you deem a successful career path for *yourself*.

Ultimately, I learned that I own my career.

If I am not happy with how work is going, I am the only person who can fix it.

If I want to make a change at work, I am the only person who can do it.

If I want to pursue a different career path, it's up to me to learn the skills necessary to make the switch.

I am not the victim of my career. I am the owner. I make the calls, the choices, and the decisions.

I'm lucky enough to have made this discovery early on in my career. Many others are not so lucky, and they fall victim to working jobs they hate because they need the money or aren't open to auditing their situation and owning the change.

This doesn't have to be you.

Building a Purpose-Driven Career

If you're ready to break the corporate blueprint and build your own ladder, you've come to the right place. You *can* find happiness and purpose in your career, whether it's working a corporate job or forging your own path. Navigating your career is challenging in all phases of life, but with the right tools you can empower yourself to make the necessary changes to finally find that satisfaction you seek, whatever it means to you.

Throughout this book, I walk you through my own corporate journey and how I ultimately took a leap of faith by leaving my corporate career and diving head-first into my own business. From feeling completely lost and unhappy on a career path that I spent years of my life preparing for, to ultimately utilizing the skills I learned to build a seven-figure business, I share every lesson I learned along the way that helped me build my own ladder.

Own Your Career is your blueprint for taking your professional power back and developing your own unique career path. Whether you plan to climb the corporate ladder or hope to "break free" and pursue a business of your own, by the end of this book, you'll be equipped with the tools you need to succeed and find happiness in the workplace. Let's dive in!

Chapter 1
Are You Lost?

Your dream job doesn't exist. If there was a single piece of advice I wish I had known the day I started my first job out of college, it's this. Young adults are not prepared for "real life." No amount of internships or college classes can equip you for the realities that are corporate America and the working world. It's a tough lesson to learn, but once you realize it, you're ready to take your career to the next level.

The Nine-to-Five Fallacy

It's likely you grew up with an idea of what your dream job would be. For me, I always thought I'd be a lawyer or a doctor or something very professional and highly regarded. This is because I was told in school that I was smart and capable, and the results spoke for themselves: I got straight As, I rarely struggled, and I didn't have a hard time getting into the college of my choice. Because of my academic experience, I figured it only made sense for me to pursue an elite career path. I had no idea what it actually took to enter these fields.

College humbled me. Straight As weren't easy anymore.

The thought of taking a college-level science class? *Hell no.*

The idea of struggling through a political history class with 48 hours' worth of reading a week? *Not a chance.*

5

I ended up choosing business—finance, specifically. Money has always been my thing. Not only were my classes interesting, but the information came easily to me. I loved the numbers, I loved working in Excel, and I loved sitting in the finance lab watching the trading board flash stock prices while I did my homework.

In the fall semester of my senior year, I landed my first postgrad job. I had done a few different internships over the course of my college career, so I thought I knew everything. I'd interned in various sectors of the finance industry, I interviewed for a handful of different jobs, and I was psyched to score—what I thought was—my dream job.

It was at a huge financial firm based in downtown Boston. I had to dress professionally every day. I was *important*. I was going to be living the dream.

TL;DR: It was not dreamy. I did not have a good time.

In this chapter, I share some of the most important lessons I learned from this job experience, along with the tumultuous career journey I experienced that transformed the way I approach work.

Lesson 1: No One Knows What They're Doing

This was the most surprising realization for me. At first, I figured it was unique to the company. *Maybe the culture there was lackadaisical, and I just ended up in a fluke department.* But this wasn't the case. Throughout my next two jobs, I noticed similar patterns. The "adults" who I always looked to for guidance and advice? They were just making things up as they went.

I always thought that everyone around me was smarter, more capable, and knew so much more than me. I spent a lot of time thinking that I was hired by mistake; *maybe I am just good at interviewing and making other people think I'm smart, when really, I'm just an idiot.*

But the truth is that no one has any idea what's going on, or what they're doing. It doesn't matter if it's your first year working or if you've been on the grind for more than 10 years: if you don't know the answer or the solution . . . just make it up.

My best advice? Stop pretending you know what you're doing. You and I both know that you're making things up as you go and hoping no one notices. Thinking that anyone else knows what's going on is an illusion, and it's causing you to doubt your own capabilities.

Lesson 2: Your Job Is Only One Part of Your Life

It is not your whole life! A nine-to-five job requires more time than simply the hours between 9 a.m. and 5 p.m. More often than not, there is at least one hour of the day for the commute, plus the time spent before and after both preparing for, and unwinding from, the workday.

Do the math: if you're awake from 7 a.m. to 10 p.m. on any given day, it's likely your schedule looks something along the lines of this:

7:00–8:30 a.m.: Wake up, coffee, get dressed, pack your bag, eat breakfast. You're doing all the necessary things to get ready for the day.
8:30–9:00 a.m.: Commute to work (assuming you have a short commute).
9:00 a.m.–5 p.m.: Work.
5:00–5:30 p.m.: Commute home.
5:30–7:00 p.m.: Exercise/some type of self-care activity.
7:00–8:00 p.m.: Shower, eat dinner.
8:00–10:00 p.m.: Relax.

Essentially, you only have about two hours a day for your own personal time. With the aftermath of the pandemic, luckily work from home has become a much more normalized practice, eliminating the commute and gifting some time back into the day for personal endeavors.

However, utilizing that personal time outside of a nine-to-five can be challenging for a few reasons. One being that many nine-to-five jobs are not actually nine-to-five; oftentimes they can look more like an eight-to-six or even a seven-to-seven, depending on your line of work.

Beyond that, working is exhausting. It's normal to feel mentally and physically wiped after a long day, whether you were in the office or not. This means that using that small amount of free time that you do have to nurture relationships, focus on a side hustle, or dedicate to personal hobbies is even harder.

I struggled finding purpose outside of my job for many years. A disproportionate amount of my life revolved around work: I lived in the city where my office was, my gym was around the corner, and many of my friends were coworkers. I found that in the few hours of personal time that I did have, I spent watching TV because I was so tired.

I fell into a trance: every day felt the same, and I wasn't working toward anything tangible. All of my life I had always been working toward the next big thing: in middle school, it was preparing for high school. In high school, it was preparing for college. In college, it was preparing to land a job.

Now I was in that job, and the next step was up to me. I was lost. I had no purpose, and I felt unstable in my life. It wasn't until I decentralized work and focused on building the life that *I* wanted that I started to feel more in control.

> Work is only one pillar of your life. If you want to have a life outside of your job, you need to treat your job as what it is: a *job,* not your everything.

Lesson 3: Nothing about Work Is Glamorous

Maybe it was just me, but I always fantasized about "working in the city" and having a big glitzy office where I got my own cubicle and had all these important "work things" to do. Growing up, I always saw adults working, but I had no idea what they were actually doing. It sounds silly, but I was excited to finally find out!

I was hit with a big, fat reality check. There is absolutely nothing glamorous about working in a big office or in a cubicle. For the first few weeks of my job, I felt so cool commuting into Boston with my work bag and my business professional clothes. I had my own cubicle, they gave me a laptop and even business cards. I felt important!

Once I actually figured out what "work" was—an endless loop of circling back, following up, touch-bases, and Kanban boards—I realized that the reality of what I thought I'd be doing and what I was actually doing were quite different.

Whether you work in a high-rise office building with floor-to-ceiling windows in a major city or in an office park in the suburbs, work is work. Sure, the environment can make things exciting at first. But after a while, the environment becomes your normal; it loses its luster and becomes mundane.

I struggled with this a lot. For my whole life, I thought that working was going to be exciting and every day was a new opportunity for me. But after a while, the days blended together, and all of a sudden, years had gone by, and I was still feeling lost and unfulfilled.

> The glamorization of work is entirely based on perception, both from what you want to be perceived as, as well as what you want others to think about you. Does it really matter if your job is perceived as being cool or important by other people if you hate what you're doing?

Lesson 4: If You Don't Own Your Career, No One Will

You are your own best advocate in the workplace. No one cares about your job and your career more than you do. Waiting for the next best opportunity to fall into your lap or for your manager to stick their neck out for you at performance review season is a sure-fire way to end up disappointed. Don't wait for others to advocate for you; advocate for yourself.

I always thought that when I felt ready for a promotion, I'd just get one. What I learned (the hard way) is that you don't get what you work for; you get what you ask for. There are a ton of strategies for this—from task-tracking to negotiation—and I will unpack all of them in detail in future chapters of this book. What you need to understand now is that you—and only you—are in the driver's seat of your career.

> If you hate your job, you have control over leaving it. If you aren't getting paid what you deserve, you have control over finding another opportunity that will pay fairly. If you're being mistreated at work, you have the choice to leave. It may not always be easy, and it may not always happen right away, but it's in your hands. Own this. Know this. And let it set you free!

Freak-Out to Freelance: My Career Transformation

At this point, you've deduced that my career journey was tumultuous. My expectations were high, and the realities of working life brought me back down to earth pretty quickly. But it wasn't all bad. I learned about myself, what I wanted my life to look like, and how to navigate tough decisions by weighing the pros and cons and the impact of every choice I made.

I'm going to walk you through a timeline of my career journey to provide some context that will be helpful throughout this book. Throughout my early career, I went through four major phases that resulted in a complete transformation of my mindset, my life, and my future.

My First Job: The Freak-Out

I graduated college in 2017 and started working a month later. This was the job I described earlier—where I was excited for the glam and ended up disappointed.

Aside from the entirely shocking reality of work that I was faced with in this job, I also realized that I was in the completely wrong role for the career path that I wanted (or *thought* I wanted, but I'll get there). The job I had accepted was quite different from the job I had thought I applied for, and the responsibilities weren't providing me with the experience I was looking for.

Looking back on this from my point of view now, I feel it is important to highlight how normal it is to be disappointed with your first job. For me, not only were my expectations too high, but I also viewed it as a make-or-break experience for my future, which it wasn't.

If you love your first job, you're in the minority. It's okay if it's not perfect, because you have plenty of time to figure out your next move. Take it for what it is and chalk it up to a learning experience.

In the early years of your career, you need to be a sponge and learn as much as possible, even if it sucks. Learn what you like, what you don't like, your communication style, how you work with others, and everything in between.

In this job, I wasn't able to learn much. The work was slow and boring, and the leadership was lacking. This resulted in a personal freak-out, because I am a doer. So to be around other people who weren't doers, and who also were in control of the experience that I had access to, sent me spiraling.

To put it lightly, I panicked. I thought that I was wasting my time and I'd never be able to find another job because everyone else was going to be two steps ahead of me while I was twiddling my thumbs waiting for my manager to assign me to a new project. I spent months in limbo trying to figure out how to address the issue: Do I speak up, do I find a new job, or do I use the time to focus on something else that will help me get my foot out the door?

This was my first experience with this, so I didn't know what the right answer was and I was afraid to make a mistake.

One of my strengths is that I always tend to channel panic into productivity and staying busy. I'm a problem solver, and once I set my mind to something, I'm going to find a way to make it happen. In typical Michela fashion, I ended up signing up for one of the hardest financial exams that exists: The CFA exam. In my mind, this was my ticket out of my current role and into a role that was more suited to the path I wanted to be on.

I started studying for it around the clock, hoping it would help me feel more in control of my career and ultimately my life. This was the doer in me; if I could fill my time doing things that felt productive, then I was moving in the right direction, right? Right.

Any uncertainty I felt was redirected into studying: the recommended study time for this exam was 300 hours, and I probably studied for closer to 500 out of sheer panic and anxiety.

Ultimately, I passed the exam (Level 1 out of 3, to be specific). This aligned closely with my next career move, where I was finally able to break into the investment industry and land the next version of "my dream job." Which, at this point you know isn't real. I just hadn't figured it out yet.

If you're in the "freak-out" phase of your career, don't worry, it's normal. Everyone goes through a period in their first or second job where they question if they've made terrible life decisions and feel totally out of control of their circumstance. It's basically a rite of passage for your early 20s.

The key is to identify that you're in this phase and start thinking about ways to address it. Assess your options: Can you make changes in your current role? Would it be more productive to find a new role? Is there an experience or knowledge gap between where you are now and where you want to be? Are you able to fill the gap with a course, a certification, or something else?

Channel the panic into problem-solving. Lay out your options, and take action from there.

My Second Job: The Quarter-Life Crisis

I struggled a lot in my first job. But my second job? It got worse. At this point, I was two years into my career, had devoted nearly an entire year to studying for an exam, and finally landed a job in the industry that I wanted.

This role was in investment consulting, which meant I was working with clients directly and helping to manage their investment portfolios. The clients I worked with were institutional, and I had line of sight into how millions of dollars were invested and allocated for optimal long-term performance. I learned immensely about investing— how to make investment decisions, how to research and evaluate different investment opportunities, and everything in between.

It was information that was applicable to my own life, and I slowly began to realize that I could take what I was learning at work and apply it to my personal finances. It lit a small fire inside of me, but I didn't have much time to explore it because I was so busy working.

My work experience in this job was entirely different from my previous one. I had significantly more responsibility, to the point where the adjustment was so brutal that I questioned why I ever wanted to change jobs in the first place. I was working long hours; 10- to 12-hour days became the norm.

I had to balance more responsibilities and work than I ever had in the past. I was the point of contact for 12 different clients who all had different personalities, goals, communication styles, and expectations. It was incredibly difficult for me to manage my time, keep track of the various expectations and timelines, while also maintaining a professional demeanor and managing my relationship with the internal team and my manager. I learned pretty quickly that client-facing roles were not my strong suit or my interest.

Remember earlier in this chapter when I highlighted that your first job doesn't have to be perfect as long as you're learning? Well, in this case it was my second job that highlighted this very valuable information that I wouldn't have learned otherwise: client-facing roles are not for me.

It was during this experience that I entered my quarter-life crisis. What was I doing? Every day I woke up and hated my life. I dreaded all of the work that hung over me. I knew when I walked into the office what was waiting: a passive-aggressive email from either a client or someone on my team, feedback on a presentation that said "pls fix," and an endless to-do list of follow-ups, circling back, and asking other people to run reports for me that I couldn't do myself.

It was exhausting. And I was reaching a point of defeat. I worked incredibly hard to get to this position, thinking that it was the solution to my career woes and I'd finally be happy, only to realize that what I thought I wanted was exactly what I *definitely* don't want, and now I need to find my way out, again.

There is a key difference between the freak-out phase and the quarter-life crisis phase. In the freak-out, you have hope. Once you hit your quarter-life crisis phase, the reality of your future of work has sunk in. It probably isn't going to get better, so now it's time to figure out how to cope so that you don't spend the next 40 years of your working life in perpetual misery.

A *quarter-life crisis* is a period of uncertainty, stress, and soul-searching that many people face somewhere in their mid- to late-twenties. It spans all areas of your life but can be exacerbated by unhappiness in your career. When you think about it, you spend a huge amount of time at work. If you're unhappy in other areas of your life *and* at your job, the directionless feeling can become overwhelming.

I addressed my quarter-life crisis by channeling my frustration at work into a new passion project: Break Your Budget. (You will learn more about Break Your Budget and my journey starting and scaling what was once a side hustle and is now my full-time job in Chapter 7.) For now, here's what you need to know: at its inception, Break Your Budget was my outlet for sharing what I was learning at work and how I was managing my own finances with the masses. I knew I was learning information that many people either didn't have access to or didn't understand, and that there was—and still is—a huge knowledge gap when it comes to financial literacy and investing.

And so I spent my time every day after work posting on Instagram what I learned and what I spent. At first, nothing really came of it. But as you can probably figure out now, it's become so much more.

My Third Job: The Turning Point

I didn't last a full year in my second job. I made it for 11 months, but I couldn't stick it out any longer. I decided to leverage the transferable skills I had learned in both of my jobs to land another type of job: corporate finance.

This job began in March of 2020, right at the beginning of the global pandemic that shut the world down. As a result, I started this job working from home at my parents' house with the intent of going into the office within the first few months when everything "went back to normal."

You know how that turned out—two weeks turned into two months, which turned into two years. I ended up moving permanently into my parents' house and spent the next year working from home while also working on Break Your Budget.

The silver lining of the pandemic was the gift of free time. I had so much time back since I wasn't commuting and my social life was essentially nonexistent. I took advantage of it by focusing on my side hustle because I can't sit still—you know, it's the doer in me. I started taking one-on-one budgeting clients, I created products and courses for sale, and I jumped on TikTok to grow my audience.

The corporate job I was working at this point in time wasn't as miserable as my first two. It was still work, but it was far more interesting and more aligned with my personal passions and vision for my career. I finally felt like I found a groove with work, and it was really refreshing despite the world collapsing all around me.

Even though the first year of the pandemic was emotionally and mentally taxing, my career was starting to fall into place. I was mostly happy at work, my side hustle was generating some extra spending cash, and I felt as if I hit my turning point. Things were getting better, and I started to feel some hope again that maybe I wouldn't be miserable forever.

In the summer of 2021, I decided to pack up and move across the country to California. The world was opening up again, and I needed to figure out what my next move would be since I couldn't live at home forever. At this point I was ready for a big change, so I booked a one-way ticket to LA, and the rest is history.

The turning point phase of your career is where you start to see the light at the end of the tunnel. You've freaked out about the reality of work, you've adjusted to life outside of the education system, you've navigated your quarter-life crisis, and now you've begun to settle into a more stable period of life.

Once I found stability in my career, I was able to view my life decisions with more clarity. It made it a lot easier for me to decide to move across the country and have faith that things would work out.

My Fourth Job: New Normal

My decision to move to Los Angeles changed my life in ways I could have never imagined. After six months of working my corporate job from LA, Break Your Budget had taken off to the point where I was ready to dive in, head first.

I quit my corporate job in March of 2022, and I've never looked back. I took a chance on myself that has paid dividends in both my career and my life. I finally found my new normal, which was the result of a major transformation in the way that I view and approach work.

Throughout those first three jobs that spanned just under five years, I learned enormously about myself, what I wanted my life to look like, and the part my career played in that equation. Some of the valuable lessons I learned include:

- A job that sounds good on paper might suck in reality.
- It doesn't matter what anyone else thinks about your job; what matters is that you like it.
- There is abundant opportunity out there if you're willing to go looking for it and put your ego and doubts aside.
- I have full and complete control over my life. My career is my choice. My circumstance is up to me. My happiness is directly correlated with the boundaries I set.

Now, I finally feel happy. Obviously, happiness is a journey, and I still experience waves of panic and occasionally find myself having a momentary freak-out, but objectively I've landed in the career that's meant for me.

And you will, too. Throughout this book I am going to unpack exactly how you can take your power back and own your career. The chapters that follow provide practical strategies, expert advice, and real-life lessons that will take you through your own career transformation. The only requirement is that you *own it*. Are you ready?

Key Takeaways

- Your dream job doesn't exist. The sooner you accept this, the easier it will be to find true satisfaction at work.
- Our culture is designed for you to revolve your life around work. You need to take intentional time to find purpose outside of your job through nurturing relationships, developing personal hobbies, or pursuing a side hustle or business idea that fuels your passion.
- The glamorization of work is based on perception. Focus on finding a job you actually enjoy doing rather than finding a job that looks or sounds cool from the outside.
- You own your career! You are your own best advocate at work—don't wait for others to advocate for you.
- The best way to approach work in your early 20s is to be a sponge. Learn as much as you can to discover what you enjoy doing, what you don't like doing, how to communicate and work with others, and everything in between. You have plenty of time.
- It's normal to experience a freak-out phase and quarter-life crisis throughout your 20s. You will find the light at the end of the tunnel and experience a turning point, eventually landing in a job you enjoy or that provides the career satisfaction you seek. Trust the process.

Chapter 2
Don't Just Increase Your Earnings

In my second job after college I took a pay cut. I distinctly remember the phone call with the HR department:

"We can offer you a salary of $60,000 per year with the opportunity to earn up to a 10% bonus."

My mind was scrambling to find the right response to this in an instant. "$60,000?" I thought. "That's less than what I'm earning right now!"

At that moment, all I could muster up was: "Can you guarantee the bonus?"

She said yes. In my mind that meant I was making $66,000 per year, and I was okay with that.

Why am I telling you this? Because during that conversation, I was looking at this job transition as an entirely transactional exchange. I had two years of work experience under my belt, so the way I thought about it, I should be making more money in my second job than in my first job.

This is a logical thought process: the more experience you have, the more you should earn. However, early in your career, which is where I was at this point in time, there is more to a job than just the salary.

Yes, you need to be getting paid a livable wage so you can pay your bills and save and do all the things. If you aren't being paid enough to comfortably live, you'll resent your job and your company even if it's providing you with valuable experience. On the other hand, you also need to be building *human capital* and making decisions that will help you increase your earning potential long-term, rather than a simple short-term gain.

In this chapter, I break down how to maximize your earning potential and how to navigate important career decisions so you get the most out of work.

Consider Your Earning Potential

A few hours after this conversation with HR, where I verbally accepted the offer in a state of sheer panic, I called my dad and told him about the situation. He is always able to talk me off a ledge and provide wisdom and perspective that I usually overlook.

This conversation is where I first discovered the concept of *earning potential*. Let me break down the thought process I had at that moment.

The job I was leaving was a dead-end job. Sure, I was getting paid a few thousand more dollars annually, but I wasn't learning anything. The work was inconsistent and uninteresting, the culture of the company was lackadaisical, and I didn't like what I was doing. I knew there was no future there for me, which is why I had been looking for a new job in the first place.

This new offer was one I had worked really hard for, and it was in an industry that I wanted to (well, *thought* I wanted to) work in. The opportunity and experience the job would provide for me was exceptional.

I'd have opportunities to network, learn new skills, work directly with clients, make investment decisions, and so much more. It would allow me to break into a new industry and open up doors that could enable me to have a lasting and successful career long-term.

When I frame it up like that, it sounds like a no-brainer to take the job that provides the better experience even though they offered less money.

This is decision-making based on earning potential. Looking at these two scenarios, I had two choices:

- Prioritize short-term earnings over long-term career gains
- Make a short-term sacrifice for a potential long-term gain

The lesson that I learned from the experience was that when evaluating a job-related decision, you need to look at the entire picture. It's important to look at the trajectory of the decision as much as the current circumstance.

A good trajectory—in my case, the new job—wouldn't increase my earnings right away. But it would absolutely increase my earnings long-term by putting me in a position to learn more and be in the room with important people who could open the door to opportunities I otherwise wouldn't have had access to. These factors help increase my *human capital*, which is a critical aspect of career success and longevity.

As a result, this would increase my earning potential significantly over the course of my career.

I chose to make a short-term sacrifice for long-term career gains. Nearly four years later, I can confirm with certainty that this was the right decision.

What Is Earning Potential?

Earning potential refers to the amount of money that an individual is capable of making over the course of their career. It's influenced by a variety of factors, including but not limited to education levels, skill set, work experience, industry, and location.

Let's dive a bit deeper on some of these factors that can influence your earning potential.

- **Education:** Higher levels of education and specialized training, including specific certifications, programs, or postgraduate education, can have a huge impact on your total compensation.
- **Skill set:** Having specialized skills within a specific industry or possessing in-demand transferable skills that can be used in

a variety of industries, roles, and companies can make you an asset in the workplace. The value of your different skills vary depending on the industry and role you are working in.

- **Industry:** Different industries have different opportunities, roles, and salary ranges at varying levels of your career. For example, an entry-level job in the communications industry oftentimes pays far less than an entry level job in the finance industry.
- **Location:** Cost of living varies depending on where you live and your compensation will likely reflect that. If you live in a higher cost of living area, you may be paid more for the same role compared to a lower cost living area (think NYC vs. Cincinnati).
- **Work experience:** This includes not only the years of work experience you have under your belt, but the range and depth of experience as well. Various responsibilities and projects that you've performed in previous jobs as well as the proficiency in skills related to these responsibilities all play a huge role in your earning potential.

When evaluating different career opportunities, you need to consider the impact they could have on your earning potential. You increase your earning potential by choosing the opportunities that allow you to grow the most, not necessarily the ones that pay the most.

Learning versus Earning

On the theme of evaluating career opportunities, let's talk about learning and earning on the job. To be cut and dry, every job or position you hold throughout your career should allow you to either learn or earn. Ideally, the job you hold will help you do both: learn a lot and gain great experience while also earning a fair wage where you can pay your bills and thrive as an adult.

Unfortunately in the world we live in today, most jobs usually offer one or the other. Therefore, when thinking about any type of career opportunity, you need to decide if it will be one where you learn or earn.

Looking back at my original example, when I decided to take the pay cut and pursue a new opportunity, the decision to *learn* was clear. I was entering a chapter of my career where making money wasn't necessarily the main goal: learning was. I needed to get a specific type of experience to move into an industry that I knew very little about. The long-term goal was then to leverage that experience for higher-paying opportunities down the line.

> Remember, every job or position you hold throughout your career should allow you to learn and/or earn.

The concept of "learning versus earning" refers to the idea that you, as an individual in the workforce, need to balance the pursuit of education, experience, and skill development with the need to earn a reasonable living. Essentially, it's the trade-off between investing your time, energy, and resources in developing human capital, or spending that same time earning money.

Human Capital: The Value of Experience

I've been throwing the term "human capital" around a lot, so let's talk about it. Human capital is the collective skills, knowledge, experience, and abilities that you possess and are able to perform within the workforce.

It goes beyond your hard skills and encompasses the value that you bring to the table at work. For example, a hard skill would be your proficiency in using a software system such as Excel. This skill contributes to your human capital but is improved on by your ability to take that skill even further, let's say by leveraging it to solve a business problem, present data that enables business decision-making, or lead to an increase in revenue.

Your ability to do this stems from formal education, prior on-the-job experience, and personal qualities such as work ethic, adaptability, creativity, and problem-solving skills. It also includes your personal experience outside of the workplace, because your ability to approach a variety of scenarios is influenced by your unique perspective. This can be formed through how you were raised, your hobbies, travel you've done, volunteer work, and so much more.

See what I am getting at here?

> Human capital is more than your repertoire of skills. It's how you implement those skills, approach your work, interact with others, share your perspective, and enable the team you work on, or company you work at, to succeed. You build human capital by gaining a variety of work and life experience, and this takes time.

In the context of the learning-versus-earning debate, human capital is an essential aspect of *learning*. Oftentimes, especially early in your career, the benefit of prioritizing learning and building human capital far outweighs the additional few thousand dollars you can earn in an alternate role. That being said, each opportunity needs to be weighed individually.

How to Build Human Capital

Building human capital involves a combination of formal education, on-the-job training, and personal development—both inside and outside of the workplace. The goal is to create your own personal portfolio of unique skills, characteristics, and experiences that make you, *you*.

With this experience, you bring your own unique perspective to the organization, which is an invaluable resource for business. Let's look at some ways you can build human capital.

Personal Life Examples of Human Capital

If you are early in your career, you may not have a ton of work experience to leverage as you build human capital. Don't worry, because you likely have some personal life experience that makes your perspective in the workplace unique.

- **Volunteer work:** Volunteering for nonprofits or community groups can provide you with opportunities to learn about different cultures and socioeconomic groups. You can gain new perspectives from others who have different life experiences than you. This can help you expand your network and develop relationships with individuals who could provide job leads or opportunities in the future.

  You can learn new skills such as fundraising, community building and outreach, and event planning, which are skills that can be applied to a variety of jobs and make you a more attractive candidate in the workplace. Volunteering also demonstrates a commitment to social responsibility and community impact, which makes you a more well-rounded person. This can be especially helpful if you are a new graduate or are looking to change careers or industries.

- **Traveling:** Traveling and experiencing different countries, cultures, and people can help you develop a global perspective and gain exposure to different ways of thinking and problem-solving. Experiencing new cultures, ideas, and perspectives that you have not encountered before broadens your understanding of the world while simultaneously helping you develop skills in both adaptability and problem-solving.

  When you are in a new environment, you need to adapt to different customs, communicate in new ways by navigating different languages or culture norms, and work with others to solve problems or complete tasks. These experiences help you develop strong interpersonal skills to succeed in the workplace.

- **Pursuing hobbies:** Pursuing your hobbies and interests outside of work can help you develop new skills and knowledge that you can transfer to your career. For example, I started Break Your Budget as a side hobby outside of my nine-to-five job and learned about social media, marketing, copywriting, sales strategy, and so much more. These are skills that I never would have learned at work.

Having a hobby can also help enhance your creativity, develop new ways of thinking, and improve your time management and organization skills, all of which are incredibly valuable in the workplace.

Workplace Examples of Human Capital

Every experience you have at work builds human capital in one way or another, whether it be specific projects you work on, people you work with, or industries you work in. Developing skills at work that can be leveraged across a variety of roles and jobs enhances your ability to increase your human capital.

- **Training and development programs:** Many organizations offer free training or development programs for employees that will help them either acquire new skills or hone and improve existing skills. This is an excellent way to learn new technical skills such as different software, business methods or techniques, and measurable abilities such as project management, public speaking, or data analysis.
- **Networking and mentorship:** Building your network can help you develop new relationships with other professionals in your industry, which can ultimately lead to new job opportunities or partnerships in the future. You can also leverage your network for opportunities to learn and seek out mentorship from individuals who are in positions you aspire to. Mentors can provide insight and advice based on their own experience while also helping guide you and identify opportunities for growth.

   Your network is your net worth in your career. Have you ever heard the saying "It's not what you know; it's who you know"? This holds true for many opportunities in the workplace, so take it seriously!
- **Industry-specific training and certifications:** Many industries require specialized training or certifications in order to

advance. For example, within the investment industry that I was working in, pursuing a CFA (Chartered Financial Analyst) designation was desirable in the eyes of employers. As a result, I began working toward the charter and passed the first of three exams. Before I decided to change careers, I was able to leverage this experience and knowledge to obtain my next job. Taking time to identify professional certifications or training that relates to your industry demonstrates to employers that you have a deep understanding of a particular skill or subject matter.

- **Seeking new responsibilities:** Taking on new projects or challenges allows you to develop new skills and knowledge that you may not have otherwise had access to. It also demonstrates that you take initiative, are proactive, and are willing to adapt to various situations, which shows employers that you are a self-starter who is capable of taking on new challenges.

Building human capital involves a commitment to learning and developing, both inside and outside of the workplace. When you show a commitment to improving yourself and your skill set alongside broadening your experience and perspective, you become a valuable asset in the job market and enhance your long-term employability.

Earning: How Much Is Enough?

Now, let's pivot the conversation back to *earning* at work. Valuable work experience is obviously important, but so is making enough money to pay your bills. The entire reason we go to work in the first place is to make money, so a livable wage is arguably *the most* (but not only) important aspect of a job.

There are three components that make up an ideal salary:

- **It's enough money to comfortably pay your bills:** It costs money to live, and your income from your job should be enough to pay your basic bills such as rent, insurance, groceries, and transportation. This is the baseline: if your salary doesn't cover the basics, you need to find a different job.

- **You can work toward financial goals:** Saving and investing for the future while paying off debt is essential to building a solid financial foundation. Thinking of your future self and setting yourself up for financial success needs to be top of mind when evaluating a job offer and deciding if a salary is "enough."
- **Spending money on non-essentials (within reason) isn't stressful:** You work hard for your money, and you should be able to enjoy it. In an ideal state, you'd not only be earning enough to pay your bills and work toward future goals but also be able to splurge on a dinner out or a piece of clothing without worrying about over-drafting your account.

It's not accurate or reasonable to say that earning in the workplace is more valuable than learning. But earning is important because you need to meet your basic needs, create a sense of security and stability, and enjoy your life.

Obviously everyone wants to make as much money as possible by doing the least amount of work necessary. However, this isn't really plausible or realistic, especially if you are new to the workforce or in your 20s and early 30s. Huge salaries tend to come along with advanced or executive titles, and those require years of experience that you simply don't have when you first start working.

That being said, starting your career off with a high salary has a ton of benefits and can positively affect your long-term earning success for several reasons.

- **Ability to save and invest:** If you start saving and investing early, your money has more time to compound. Compound interest (see the sidebar) is the concept of your money earning more money on itself; I discuss this concept at length in my book *Own Your Money*. The key to saving and investing early is to have the discretionary income to do so, which means you need to be earning a high salary. This can lead to long-term financial security as well as the ability to pursue opportunities without money being the driving decision-maker.
- **Negotiation power:** A higher starting salary can give you negotiating power for future salary increases. The higher you

start, in theory, the higher you can go. This holds especially true if you have specialized experience, an advanced degree, or professional certification that is in high demand.

- **Increased confidence:** This is an intangible benefit of starting your career with a high salary. While I don't condone associating your self-worth with your salary, it can absolutely boost your confidence and make it easier to believe in your abilities and skills early on. This can translate to a greater willingness to take risks, pursue new opportunities, and negotiate for higher salaries and benefits in the future. This holds especially true if you are able to leverage that high salary to build a solid financial foundation and do not have to worry about living paycheck to paycheck or making ends meet every month.

Earning a high salary in your 20s is dependent on a variety of factors, including the area you choose to live in, the role and industry you choose to work in, as well as the job market and economy at the time you apply. When evaluating an opportunity, consider the impact the compensation package can have on your quality of life, and ensure that you are being paid a wage that will support your basic needs.

Compound Interest Explained

Compound interest has been deemed "the eighth wonder of the world" by Albert Einstein, and for good reason. It refers to the concept of your money earning money on itself. When you contribute money to an interest-bearing account such as an investment account or a high-yield savings account, that money has the opportunity to earn interest. Over time, as you accumulate interest, you begin to earn interest not only on the initial money you contributed (called the *principal*) but also on the interest you've earned on that principal. This leads to exponential growth and allows your money to work for you by generating substantial returns over the long term.

The Great Debate: To Learn or to Earn?

It's clear that learning and earning go hand in hand when evaluating career opportunities. The balance between the two is a personal decision that depends on a variety of situational factors, including financial stability, career goals, and personal interests.

The exciting (or scary, depending how you look at it) part of your post-graduate experience is that every decision you make influences the direction both your career and your life can go, and it's entirely up to you!

Up until this point, your big life decisions were made for you. You were required to go to school, likely told to go to college, and are now funneled into society in the form of entering the workforce and landing a job. From this point on, you get to decide your next move and prioritize what is most important to you, and *only you*.

As a now late-twenty-something, I love to look back and see where my peers from high school and college have landed since graduation. Every single person has branched off in a different direction: some to grad school, others to a steady corporate job, and others to marriage and family. Everyone has made personal decisions based on their needs, wants, and desires for their own future.

When it comes to working, you get to choose what you prioritize. You may want to start by prioritizing learning, whether it be through on-the-job experience or by pursuing graduate education. This could mean sacrificing some income in the short term in order to gain the skills and knowledge necessary to advance your career, as we discussed in our conversation around human capital.

On the other hand, you could instead prioritize earning, focusing on landing a high-paying job so you can build financial stability, travel without worry, or maybe retire early.

When evaluating career decisions, you need to be strategic about the opportunities you pursue and weigh your ability to both learn and earn. This could mean pursuing jobs in industries where you have opportunities to do both, or nursing career paths and advanced degrees that have a clear path to earning a high salary.

Here are a few questions to ask yourself when you are making a career decision:

- *What are my current values and priorities? How do I see these changing in the next one, five, and ten years?* Consider what is most important to you in both your personal and professional life currently, and the vision you hope for yourself in the future. How does this opportunity align?
- *What salary and benefits are important to me?* Consider your current and future financial goals and needs, as well as the benefits that are important to you. Maybe the offer includes a high salary but minimal 401(k) and insurance benefits, and that is not appealing to you. Or maybe you have a solid savings account to fall back on, and you are ready to compromise your compensation to get your hands dirty and learn a lot. I discuss compensation packages in detail as well as navigating these decisions in Chapter 5.
- *What opportunities can I gain from this experience, and how will it help me advance my career?* Consider the experience you'll gain on the job, from actual project-based opportunities to networking and career development opportunities. Evaluate if you will be able to take formal trainings, develop skills, learn new specialized knowledge, or grow your network.

These three questions cover the strategic areas of any career-related decision: your personal values, your ability to earn, and your ability to learn. Rank them in order of priority each time you reach a point of pivotal decision-making, so you can decide what is most and least important to you at that time.

Ultimately, the balance between learning and earning is delicate. It requires careful consideration of your personal priorities, circumstances, and desires for your future. It's also fluid; you will likely move through chapters of your life where you prioritize learning and others where you prioritize earning. The job market is constantly changing, and the skills and experiences that are in demand change with it. Stay agile, be flexible, focus on constant learning, and you'll naturally position yourself for both short- and long-term success.

Key Takeaways

- When you are making career-related decisions, you need to consider more than the compensation. Evaluate the impact the decision could have on your earning potential and career trajectory with just as much weight as the salary.
- Your earning potential is the amount of money you are capable of making over the course of your career and is influenced by factors such as your education level, skill set, industry, location, and work experience.
- Every job or position you hold throughout your career should allow you to learn and/or earn. Ideally, your job will do both; but if it does neither, it is time to move on to a new opportunity.
- Human capital is the collective skills, knowledge, experience, and abilities that you possess and can perform in the workforce. It is the combination of your hard skills and unique experience that shape how you approach your work.
- An ideal salary accomplishes three major goals: it's enough to comfortably pay your bills, you can work toward your financial goals, and you can spend money on non-essentials without stress.
- You get to choose what you prioritize in your career, depending on your needs and desires for your life. Consider your personal values, your ability to earn, and your ability to learn at each pivotal career moment.

Chapter 3

Resumé Secrets: Strategies for Standing Out in a Competitive Job Market

Throughout my corporate career, I have applied to nearly a thousand jobs. My strategy for every job search was to apply to as many as possible in the hopes that my resumé would stand out among all of the other applicants that I'm sure were just like me.

In today's day and age, expert advice would tell you this was a poor strategy.

"You need to leverage your network!" they say. Leveraging my network did actually land me a job, but, ironically, it landed me the one job in my career that I truly hated. Leaving that job was awkward as hell and (temporarily) affected my relationships at the time. I don't share this to scare you out of networking, but it's important to know that when you *do* leverage your network to land a job, it can be delicate.

After that experience I decided that in any future job change, I was going to find the opportunity on my own merit. It didn't mean that I was never going to leverage my network again, but I sure wasn't going to *rely* on it.

This was my way of taking my job search into my own hands. I had solid experience, and I felt confident that I could articulate that experience well in an interview. The challenge for me was never the interview (I talk about interviewing in the next chapter). *Getting the interview* is the hard part, especially when you're applying blind, and this is where a rock solid resumé comes into play.

I can confirm that the reason I landed a majority of my interviews was because my resumé was awesome. I know this because for 99% of the jobs I applied to that resulted in an interview I didn't have a connection or a reference.

This means that my resumé was distinct. Not only did it make it past the ATS (applicant tracking system), but it stood out in the seven seconds that the recruiter scanned it before deciding whether I was a good fit. As a result, I was able to get my foot in the door at some major companies such as Twitter, Liberty Mutual, and Alo Yoga *without a connection.*

The strategies I'm going to teach you in this chapter are a combination of lessons learned throughout my own experience, discussions with recruiters, and in-depth research on "the art" of writing a good resumé. By implementing the lessons you learn in this chapter, you'll be well on your way to landing tons of interviews without a single connection.

Analyzing Resumés

Austin Belcak is a pioneer in the resumé world. I wish I knew he existed when I was working corporate because the information he provides is incredibly useful. In 2021 Austin conducted a study (Cultivated Culture 2021) of the most effective resumés and whether candidates were using resumé best practices to optimize their job search.

He analyzed over 125,000 resumés to answer a single question: *How many candidates are following best practices, and where are the opportunities to create a better, more effective resumé?*

The following sections break down his key findings.

Key Finding 1: LinkedIn Can Help You Secure an Interview

LinkedIn has grown in popularity over the last few years, especially as Gen Z has begun to enter the workforce. According to the study, "Resumés with a LinkedIn profile see higher interview rates, but only 48% of resumés included a LinkedIn profile."

LinkedIn is the largest professional network in the world, so it comes as no surprise that utilizing the platform can help during the job application process. In fact, you can even apply for jobs directly on LinkedIn, see how many other applicants are interested in the opportunity, and connect directly with the recruiter.

The potential upsides to utilizing LinkedIn are obvious, but many job seekers still don't use the platform to its full extent. According to Peter Yang, the CEO of ResumeGo, applicants who included a link to their LinkedIn profile saw an increased callback rate on their applications. The callback rate was 7.2% for those who had a "bare-bones" LinkedIn profile, and 13.5% for those who had a comprehensive LinkedIn profile on their resumé (ResumeGo n.d.).

The key word here is *comprehensive*. What constitutes a comprehensive LinkedIn profile that will actually make a difference? These were profiles that "had profile summaries of over 1000 characters, 300 connections or more, dense bullet-point or paragraph-based descriptions for every work experience section listed, and a professional headshot" (ResumeGo n.d.). Creating a profile defined as "comprehensive" takes considerable time but can also show employers that you are serious about your job search.

Darci Smith, who is a professional recruiter and Partner at Roklyn Consulting, corroborated this observation. She described your LinkedIn page as your "portfolio." You can leverage the About Me section to "show a little bit more of your human side and what you're passionate about. You can definitely focus your efforts more toward the industry that you're applying to, [recruiters] can see the connections that you have, and that goes a long way," she states.

> Check out my interview with Darci Smith on my podcast at `https://podcasters.spotify.com/pod/show/breakyourbudget`.

Let's break this advice down into steps you can implement:

Step 1: Write a detailed profile summary. One thousand characters is approximately one paragraph or five to seven sentences. You want to highlight your expertise, an example of profound or significant work you've done, a personal interest, and what you are seeking in your job search or career.

Step 2: Grow your network. Make sure you send connection requests to your peers from high school and college, coworkers, and any other connection you may have in your network. Not only does this establish credibility on your profile, but it can also open you up to opportunities and new connections in your network's network.

Step 3: Highlight your job experience. Rather than including just your job title and company for each job experience on your profile, include bullet points that highlight the experience from each role. They can be condensed versions of your resumé bullet points and should emphasize major projects or skills you learned in that particular job.

Step 4: Add a professional headshot. Your LinkedIn headshot needs to be recent and reflective of *what you actually look like right now*. If you've been out of college for five years, you should not be using a graduation photo. Many companies will take your headshot at work for free, so ask your HR department if this service exists. Otherwise, you can take a professional headshot using Portrait Mode on your iPhone.

The major takeaway is that utilizing a tool such as LinkedIn and including it on your resumé can drastically improve your chances of landing an interview. This isn't a tactic I personally utilized in my own job searching process, but if I were to begin applying to jobs again today, I absolutely would leverage LinkedIn.

Key Finding 2: Include Keywords and Skills That Match the Job Description

This doesn't necessarily mean that your current experience has to exactly match the job description you are applying for. It means that you need to frame your experience to align with the posting.

When you apply for a job, your resumé is filtered through an ATS (applicant tracking system), which uses keywords, skills, and experience to determine whether you are a qualified applicant. Even with relevant experience to the job, if you don't properly highlight it on your resumé based on the keywords in the description, your resumé could get sorted into the "No" pile and that opportunity is missed.

In fact, if you've ever applied to a job and submitted your resumé, and then had to resubmit each section of your resumé and additional information through an interface such as Workday, ADP, or Greenhouse, you've used an ATS system. According to Smith, the ATS is a "system for organization for the other side of the coin. Hiring teams will use [them] to be able to track applicants" as well as filter candidates based on specified criteria and keywords directly related to the role.

If your resumé makes it past the initial ATS filter, a recruiter will spend an average of seven seconds skimming it for details, according to a study conducted by Ladders in 2018 (Ladders 2018). In those seven seconds, recruiters are looking for specific skills and experience from the job description to determine whether you are a qualified applicant worthy of moving forward in their process; if those skills are not on your resumé, you will likely not move forward.

Smith notes that many hiring teams will set up the ATS with "this or that" criteria. For example, if a person has "this" skill, they'll move forward, if they don't, then they won't. This highlights the importance of keywords because the ATS system is a computer— there is no gray area, so either you fit the criteria or you don't.

Here is how you can optimize your resumé for this process:

Step 1: Research the types of jobs you are interested in. Look for common themes in experience needed, skills desired, and key-words across multiple job descriptions for similar roles. Make sure that these are incorporated in the bulk of your resumé. You can always make small tweaks for different applications.

Step 2: Incorporate keywords naturally. It's really important that your resumé reads naturally and that you don't over-index your use of keywords. Aim to include as many as three keywords per bullet within each job experience you highlight. You can also include a "Skills" section where you highlight both hard and soft skills.

Utilizing keywords and skills correctly on your resumé can make or break your success. Take the time to understand the key factors of the jobs you are applying for and optimize your resumé accordingly.

Key Finding 3: Companies Prefer Measurable Metrics and Quantifiable Results

If you take one key learning from this entire chapter, let it be this one: you need to *quantify* as much as you possibly can on your resumé. Explaining that you have a specific experience isn't enough; you need to take it one step further and highlight the *impact* or the *value* that specific experience had in the workplace.

According to Belcak's study, the minimum recommendation of measurable or quantifiable instances on a resumé is five. Only 26% of the resumés he analyzed included five or more instances of measurable metrics and 59% included three or fewer. This means if your resumé includes five or more, you have a much greater chance of standing out and showcasing the value you can bring as an employee.

Smith has an aligned perspective but with a different twist: she focuses on what she calls "low data and high data." Low data are the experiences and strengths that aren't metrics driven. Strengths could include skills such as communication and organization, while experiences could be utilizing software such as Excel or Salesforce. The goal is to pair this "low data" with "high data" that is quantifiable.

Smith defines "high data" as your success or activity metrics that drive results. A success metric would be a quantifiable result that is directly correlated to your work, for example, increasing website traffic by 30%. If you don't have success metrics or you work in a support role, you can focus on quantifiable activity metrics. These are metrics that define parameters around projects or responsibilities. For example, how long was the project you worked on, how many people do you manage, how much data have you analyzed? Think about quantifying the work you do and who or what the impact is.

By combining low data and high data, you are able to highlight your strengths and skills while simultaneously demonstrating the impact you have. You can take this one step further by using the X-Y-Z formula to format your bullet points.

Google recruiters suggest following "the X-Y-Z formula" (Murphy 2019) for writing measurable and relevant bullets on your resumé. This is described as: "Accomplished [X] as measured by [Y], by doing [Z]."

Here's how you can implement this framework:

Step 1: Highlight your top three to five major accomplishments for each job you've held. These could be related to specific projects you've worked on, processes you've improved, or skills you've learned.

Step 2: Identify measurable and quantifiable metrics for each accomplishment. The metrics don't have to be related to just dollars or sales figures. They can include scope, quantity, other team members, or efficiency. For example, in my first job I participated in a company-wide "Innovation Challenge." My team won, and this was a major highlight on my resumé.

I could have said "Winner of company-wide Innovation Challenge" but instead I said, "Awarded first place by senior leadership

for $100K Innovation Challenge from over 20 competing teams by presenting an artificial intelligence application idea." See the difference? The first example provides no context or impact. The second example highlights various quantifiable metrics that illustrate the gravity of the accomplishment following the X-Y-Z formula.
Step 3: Apply the X-Y-Z formula to each accomplishment. This is best illustrated by the following examples.

Client Support Example

Before: Grew sales and revenue for small business jewelry clients.

X-Y-Z: Increased year-over-year sales for three small business jewelry clients by 15% by implementing an automated customer acquisition system that takes clients from social media DMs into a four-sequence email marketing funnel.

Here's the breakdown:

[X] Increased year-over-year sales (low data)
[Y] for three small business jewelry clients by 15% (high data)
[Z] by implementing an automated customer acquisition system that takes clients from social media DMs into a four-sequence email marketing funnel (low and high data combined)

Data Analysis Example

Before: Prepared monthly reports to present to senior leadership.

X-Y-Z: Analyzed monthly financial data for business verticals of over $1M in recurring revenue by compiling product sales information and identifying key drivers to share with four members of executive leadership.

Here's the breakdown:

[X] Analyzed monthly financial data (low data)
[Y] for business verticals of over $1M in recurring revenue (high data)
[Z] by compiling product sales information and identifying key drivers to share with four members of executive leadership (low and high data combined)

Software Engineering Example

Before: Automated client acquisition system.

X-Y-Z: Automated client acquisition system to manage, track, and maintain relationships with over 100 current clients by writing code that captures client inquiries and sends updates based on keywords in messaging, saving the sales team 60 minutes of admin work daily.

Here's the breakdown:

[X] Automated client acquisition system (low data)
[Y] to manage, track, and maintain relationships with over 100 current clients (high data)
[Z] by writing code that captures client inquiries and sends updates based on keywords in messaging, saving the sales team 60 minutes of admin work daily (low and high data combined)

Not only does following this method showcase the measurable and quantifiable impact of your work, but it makes the process of writing bullets a lot more efficient. Don't worry if you can't quantify everything, but aim to do so for at least 50% of your bullet points.

Key Finding 4: The Ideal Resumé Is 475–600 Words

The "sweet spot" for resumés is between 475 and 600 words; in fact, resumés included in the study that fell outside of that range saw significant decreases in effectiveness at landing an interview. An important caveat to this tip is your career level. As you progress through your career, it's normal for your resumé to be longer when you highlight additional experience. According to Smith, a one-page resumé is ideal.

To assess where your resumé currently stands, here's what you can do:

Step 1: Use the word count tool on your resumé. It's likely you wrote your resumé in Microsoft Word or Google Docs (and if you used Canva, you'll need to redo your resumé anyways. We'll get there). You can use the word count tool to see where you currently stack up.

Step 2: Update your resumé to fit the parameters. Whether you are over or under, you'll need to make some adjustments. If you're under, there is likely additional work or education experience you can highlight. You could also consider adding a skills section or a career highlights section to fill the space. If you're over, use the X-Y-Z formula to hone your bullet points. Remember, you can always elaborate on certain experiences when you land the interview.

As part of this writing process, I put my resumé to the test. My resumé was 702 words, which is a bit over this recommendation but still fits within a single page. Remember that 475–600 words is a guideline, so don't fret if you are slightly over. If you're way under, there is room for you to elaborate.

Key Finding 5: Buzzwords and Fluff Can Devalue Your Resumé

According to Belcak's study, 51% of resumés include buzzwords, clichés, or incorrect pronouns, which can make your resumé less professional and harder to understand. Plus, they add additional and unnecessary words that can distract from the main point you are trying to make within each bullet. Save the fluff for the interview!

Luckily this is an easy fix.

Step 1: Look for any cliché buzzwords or phrases in your bullet points. A few examples include the words "synergy" or "bandwidth." Common phrases to avoid could include "new normal" or "bring to the table."

Step 2: Follow the X-Y-Z formula. I know I sound like a broken record, but I can't emphasize enough how important it is to be concise and highlight your value with measurable metrics. Your point will go much further following this method as opposed to trying to swoon the recruiter with buzzwords.

The major takeaway from this entire resumé study is that most candidates are not getting the basics right. As an applicant, that means in order to stand out you really don't need to do anything groundbreaking outside of nailing these few key tactics. If you take the extra time to refine your resumé, exclude any fluff, and follow the correct framework, you'll set yourself apart from the vast majority of resumés you're up against.

Crafting a Compelling Narrative

There is much debate over what the "right" resumé format should be. Some say it's better to have color and to design your resumé in an eye-catching way, while others say it's best to keep it minimal. Beyond the visual format, there is also debate around the layout and whether it should be chronological, where you should place your education, and if you need to include a skills summary or personal interest section.

The ultimate goal of your resumé is to tell your story and share your experiences as they relate to your career and a specific job. Therefore, when crafting your resumé you want to ensure that the content you include is relevant but also that the way you format and structure your experience is efficient.

First, let's talk about some resumé formatting *don'ts!*

- *Don't* **use color or any theatrical designs.** And yes, this means those aesthetic Canva templates that have background colors and funky fonts. Not only are these templates unprofessional and distracting, but they are built on text boxes and other elements that the ATS may not be able to decipher. This puts you at an unnecessary disadvantage.

  The only time color or design has a place on your resumé is if you are applying for creative roles where showcasing your creativity and skill set is encouraged. However, even in these situations it is likely you have a portfolio of work that would better showcase your talent.

- *Don't* **stray from traditional fonts.** Times New Roman, Arial, or Calibri are your best bets. Choose one and stick to it for the entire document. You do not need to have various header fonts and you should not use any heavily stylized or cursive fonts because the ATS can't read them!

- **_Don't_ include a picture or any type of graphic.** Your resumé should be text only. This means no pictures, graphics, logos, or emblems of any type. Additionally, you should not include a picture of yourself anywhere on your resumé. Not only is what you look like irrelevant to your ability to perform as an employee, but it can subject you to unintentional bias during the hiring process.
- **_Don't_ try to hide keywords.** I mentioned earlier that keywords are very important to include, but don't try to be sly and hide keywords in blank or empty areas of your resumé. A "hack" many unreliable resumé websites will tell you to do is pull keywords from the job description, add them to the bottom of your resumé and make the font white so you can't see them. This doesn't work, and if you get caught, it's a bad look.

Additional _don'ts_ (unrelated to formatting):

- **_Don't_ use an unprofessional email.** Don't use any old usernames or phrases, and make sure your email is just your name. If you need to make a new email, do it.
- **_Don't_ include your GPA.** Unless an employer specifically asks for your GPA, there is no need to include it on your resumé, especially if you graduated college more than a year ago. Once you are an adult, no one cares.
- **_Don't_ lie.** An occasional exaggeration to emphasize a skill is okay, but don't lie about your experience. This will backfire.

First impressions are everything, and your resumé is often your first impression on a recruiter during the job search. You only get one, so you don't want to blow it with basic mistakes.

Now that I've covered all the resumé don'ts, let's talk about what you should do instead!

Resumé formatting *dos*:

- *Do* **start with your work experience.** The whole point of your resumé is to showcase your work experience, so this should be front and center. The only time your work experience wouldn't go at the top is if you are either in college or recently graduated college with little to no applicable experience yet.
- *Do* **use bullet points to itemize your experience.** Paragraphs have no place on a resumé. Within each work experience you are highlighting, include three to five bullet points using the X-Y-Z formula that highlight your main accomplishments in the role. Be clear but concise because you can always elaborate in the interview.
- *Do* **aim to keep it to one page.** As discussed earlier, the optimal resumé length is 475–600 words, which is approximately one page. In the seven seconds a recruiter is scanning your resumé, the likelihood they are going to look at a second page is slim. If you have a lot of work experience, condense it or leave off any irrelevant experience to the job you are applying for.
- *Do* **keep the format consistent.** Choose one font and one header style and stick to it. Aim to keep each work description of similar length, and don't add any distracting colors, graphics, or images.
- *Do* **proofread your work.** Is there anything less professional than a typo? It shows an employer you are not paying attention to the details. Use the spelling and grammar tools that Word provides and then double-check it.

The Optimal Resumé Structure

If you're ready to overhaul your resumé, here's exactly how you can format it for the highest chance of success:

- **Start with your name and contact information at the top.** Include your full first and last name, email, and phone number. You do not need to include your mailing address.

- **List your work experience in reverse chronological order.** The first work experience listed should be your current or most recent job, and the prior jobs you've held should follow in order. Within each work experience description, include your experience in order of relevance to the job. The most applicable project or work you've done to the role you are applying to should go at the top.
- **Beneath your work experience, include your education.** Your education does not need to go at the top of your resumé unless you are a recent grad with minimal experience. Include your university and the degree you've earned. You can also include any notable scholarships or awards from your education in this section. If you haven't earned a college degree, you can leave education off your resumé entirely so as to not draw attention to it, or highlight any certificates or certifications you've earned.
- **Include any skills or certifications at the bottom.** Your skills section is where you can highlight specific, job-related skills or software you are proficient in. Again, keep the job description and the ATS in mind. According to Smith, many recruiters are scanning your resumé and simply looking for the specific skills related to the open role. If you have specific software you use in your industry, or you want to highlight your proficiency with a tool such as Excel, Power BI, Adobe, or the like, a skills section is a great place to do that.

    Using myself as an example, in my corporate career I used various software and took a handful of certification classes that I felt would help my resumé standout. These included becoming a Certified Scrum Master, passing Level 1 of the CFA Exam, and taking an Excel Certification course. I also learned how to use software such as Power BI, SAP, and Anaplan, which were all relevant to the jobs I was looking for. I grouped all of these together at the bottom and titled the section "Relevant Professional Skills."

Optional additions:

- **Include personal interests if room allows.** This is where you can add a few bullets about your hobbies or interests outside of the workplace. Including small tidbits of information about yourself can humanize you, and if you have anything in common with the recruiter, it may make it more likely that your resumé makes it through. It also provides a great opportunity for small talk in the beginning or end of an interview. Remember: people hire people!

A few examples of personal information I included on my resumé were the study abroad programs I went on in college, that I ran the Boston Marathon in 2018, and that I had a personal finance social media page. In all of the interviews that I participated in, at least one of these topics was brought up, so it's definitely worth considering if you have anything notable you'd like to share or be comfortable discussing.

According to Smith, if you're going to add personal interests, you need to be specific. For example, rather than saying that you like hiking, highlight a notable hike you've done. In my own example, rather than saying that I enjoy running, I highlighted the specific marathon I ran. If you choose to include personal interests, be strategic and ensure they are conversational.

- **Include a career highlights section.** If you are someone who is looking to pivot career paths or needs to provide some type of explanation for something on your resumé (for example, a career gap), a "Career Highlights" summary can be valuable. According to Smith, this is three bullet points at the top of your resumé highlighting key experience directly related to the job description.

Ultimately, when you are writing your resumé, the goal is to control your own narrative. Aside from including relevant information, be sure to focus on including information that you are comfortable and excited to talk about! As you continue on your career journey, remember that crafting an effective resumé is an ongoing process that requires continuous self-reflection and refinement.

If you are seeking an example resume that follows the framework described throughout this chapter, you can download a free template at www.breakyourbudget.com/downloads.

First Name Last Name
professionalemail@email.com
OPTIONAL: Phone Number

EXPERIENCE

MOST RECENT COMPANY City, State
Most Recent Role Title Month /Year - Month/Year

- Utilize the X-Y-Z Formula to highlight your top 3-5 accomplishments in each role by identifying and quantifying the impact you have had on the work or project you are referring to.
- Highlight first your accomplishment {X}, as measured by {Y} which is your quantifiable metric, by doing {Z} which is the action you took.
- The X-Y-Z Formula is the most efficient way to translate your experience to a recruiter by highlighting measurable and/or quantifiable data that shows the impact you have made at the company.
- Make sure to start each bullet point with an action verb; if you are describing work in your current role, use present tense. If you are describing work in your past role, use past tense. Make sure that within each role you are consistent.
- See below a few examples of the X-Y-Z Formula in action that you can use as a framework for your own experience.

2nd MOST RECENT COMPANY City, State
Most Recent Role Title Month /Year - Month/Year

- Analyzed monthly financial data for business verticals of over $1M in recurring revenue by compiling product sales information and identifying key drivers to share with 4 members of Executive Leadership.
- Automated client acquisition system to manage, track, and maintain relationships with over 100 current clients by writing code that captures client inquiries and sends updates based on keywords saving the sales team 60 minutes of work daily.
- Increased year-over-year sales for 3 small business jewelry clients by 15% by implementing an automated customer acquisition system that takes clients from social media DMs into an email marketing funnel.
- Streamlined internal processes by implementing a new project management system used by 30 employees, resulting in a 30% reduction in project completion time.
- Presented project findings to a 5-person cross-functional leadership team that led to the decision to launch a new product that will generate an additional $500,000 in revenue within the first quarter.

3rd MOST RECENT COMPANY City, State
Most Recent Role Title Month /Year - Month/Year

- Negotiated and secured $1M in cost savings by optimizing 10 vendor contracts and conducting competitive bidding while maintaining the quality of services.
- Implemented a social media marketing campaign by exercising 10 cross-platform posts that resulted in a 40% growth in the company's online following and contributed to a 15% increase in online sales.
- Trained and mentored a team of five new employees leading to a significant reduction in onboarding time and improved overall team performance.
  Notice how in these bullet points there are 2 types of quantifiable metrics: non-result driven metrics (10 vendor contracts, 4 members of Executive Leadership) and result-driven metrics (15% increase, $500,000 revenue).

EDUCATION

COLLEGE/UNIVERSITY Location (City/State)

Degree Earned (BA, BSBA, etc.), Major or concentration Years Attended (20XX-20XX)

- If you earned any type of scholarship, certificate, or award, highlight here.

ANY ADDITIONAL EDUCATION (Study abroad, higher Location (City/State)
degree, etc.)
Degree Earned (BA, BSBA, etc.), or program participated in Years Attended (20XX-20XX)

- If you earned any type of scholarship, certificate, or award, highlight here.

SKILLS AND PERSONAL

- Use this to highlight 2-3 keyword skills: software you use, certifications earned, industry-specific knowledge
- Add 1-2 personal interests or hobbies *that are specific!* For example, if you enjoy running, have you completed any notable races? If you enjoy travel, what is your favorite trip?

Key Takeaways

- There are five best practices for creating a compelling resumé that will increase your chances of landing an interview. They include leveraging LinkedIn, including keywords that match the job description, incorporating measurable metrics, keeping your resumé between 475 and 600 words, and avoiding using too many buzzwords and "fluff."
- A recruiter spends an average of seven seconds scanning your resumé for details to determine if you are a good fit for a specific role. This highlights the importance of creating a resumé with keywords that emphasize your skills and experience relevant to the job you are applying for.
- Incorporating measurable and quantifiable data on your resumé by using the X-Y-Z formula will highlight your strengths and demonstrate the impact you have in a clear and concise manner.
- How you format your resumé can make or break your application. Ensure that you don't include any images or logos and keep your formatting consistent with one traditional font and three to five bullet points per experience.
- The optimal resumé format includes listing your work experience in reverse chronological order, followed by your education and an optional skills/personal section toward the bottom.

Chapter 4
Interviewing for Success

Interviewing used to terrify me. In college, I was selected to interview at a huge insurance company. They flew me from Raleigh to Boston and put me up in a top floor room in the Liberty Hotel. I was one of 15 other candidates being interviewed for a competitive rotational program, and we were all in Boston for their Super Day.

If you're not familiar, a Super Day is a marathon interview day, usually held for entry-level analysts who are feeding from universities into banks, insurance companies, private equity firms, or hedge funds. It's often a four- to six-hour day that includes a handful of interviews, a lunch, and social hour for networking in a "casual" setting. To put it lightly, it was the scariest day of my life. If I wanted to land this job, I needed to step up.

I put so much pressure on myself. I spent days preparing, I got my best suit dry-cleaned, I had my sister stay with me in the hotel, and leading up to it, I could barely eat. I wanted to get the job, but really, I think I wanted to be liked and get the validation that I was smart enough to succeed in this environment.

Fast-forward, I did not get the job, which sucked. But it was an amazing lesson for me that I still carry to this day: interviewing is a mutual experience. Yes, you want the hiring team to like you.

51

But *you* also need to like the team, the role, and the company. It needs to be the right fit for both parties; it can't just be the company deciding whether you're worthy enough for them or not.

I went into this interview hoping that *they* would like me. Because of that, I was nervous, I wasn't on my A game, and I made rookie mistakes during the process that I wouldn't have made had I taken some of the pressure off. I also didn't evaluate the situation to ensure it was the right fit *for me*. Looking back knowing what I know now, it wouldn't have been the right fit even if I got the job.

Interviewing Is a Two-Way Street

As I interviewed throughout the remainder of my corporate career, I learned the secret to interview success: *You are interviewing them just as much as they are interviewing you.* If you make it past a phone screen, the company is interested in hiring you. It's in your best interest to act as if the job is already yours.

Had I learned this lesson sooner, I likely wouldn't have struggled so much between jobs. It was actually when I was in the process of deciding to leave corporate altogether that I began raking in job offers left and right.

At the beginning of 2022, I was struggling a lot at work. I didn't like my manager, and I was passed over for a promotion that I felt I deserved, but Break Your Budget was doing really well. I had no idea if I was ready to take the leap yet, but I knew I needed to get a new job, so I started to apply. At this point, I wasn't miserable in my current job, and I wasn't desperate to leave in the same ways I had been in the past. Really, I wanted to see what was out there.

After a few applications, I landed two interviews at very well-known companies, and I was psyched. I approached the interview process entirely differently this time; since I wasn't desperate to leave my current job, and because I knew I could potentially fall back on Break Your Budget, I went into the interviews with the perspective of "What could this company offer *me*?"

Was the role interesting? Did I like the people? Was the compensation and benefits package up to my standards? For me to change jobs at this point, I was looking for a major salary bump. If the company couldn't offer it, I wasn't even going to go through the process and waste my time.

Now, I want to be clear: I took the interview process very seriously, but my attitude around it was different than in the past. I was honest when I spoke to the team, I asked pointed questions about what I would actually be doing, and I wanted to hear about their experience working there—the good and the bad.

The result? I got both offers, and they were both above what I had originally asked for. Ultimately I declined both, jumped head-first into full-time entrepreneurship, and haven't looked back since. But this was an incredible turning point for me and made me realize that showing up in an interview confident in your skills and with the perspective that *you* are the one evaluating *them* put me in the driver's seat of the process.

Approaching the interview process this way has two main benefits:

- First, it shows the hiring manager and team that you are confident in your abilities and are taking ownership of the process. Many candidates show up in a job interview and try to prove that they are the one who should be chosen, and this can translate as a lack of confidence. As I mentioned earlier, if you're in the interview, they've already chosen you. Own this, and use the interview to see if *you want to choose them.*
- Second, it allows you to look at the role objectively and decide whether you actually want to work there. The interview process is an evaluation period. You are evaluating them as much as they are evaluating you; don't forget this. Ask the hard questions, look at the role from every angle, and use the interview to better understand if the job is going to be the right fit *for you.* Ultimately, if you land the job and move forward, it becomes your new reality: you need to like it!

Throughout this chapter, I'm going to teach you the best strategies for nailing your interview and increasing your odds of landing the offer. By implementing the lessons you learn in this chapter, you'll not only get more offers, but you'll be able to decipher if they're worth taking and if they are the right fit for accelerating your career.

Setting the Record Straight

Interviewing is intimidating—there is no doubt about it. The best way to reframe your approach to interviewing is to remember that it's a mutual conversation, not a one-sided interrogation.

The next sections discuss some common interview misconceptions that could prevent you from putting your best foot forward in the process.

Myth #1: Your Resumé Is Your Best Bet at Landing the Job

It's commonly thought that your resumé, a certain degree, or work experience at a desirable company will ensure lifelong career success, but this isn't true. The way you interview, how you articulate your experience, and how you conduct yourself throughout the process holds far more weight than a fancy degree or prior job title.

A strong resumé or a connection can get your foot in the door, but the interview is where you get the job. You need to be personable, articulate, and communicate your values clearly in person. Even if you are the stand-out candidate on paper, if you blow the interview, you won't get the job. People hire people!

Myth #2: The Interviewer Knows What They Are Doing

The interviewer—usually, the hiring manager—is just another person who is likely juggling a lot of other responsibilities beyond conducting your interview. You have no idea what they were doing before or what they need to do after the conversation.

The reality is that you have likely spent much more time preparing for this interview than the interviewer. It's also likely that any person who is interviewing you beyond HR doesn't have a ton of experience conducting interviews. They could be just as nervous as you are! Remember that the person on the other side of the conversation is also just a person who was sitting in your position at some point.

Myth #3: The Most Qualified Person Will Get the Job

The unfortunate reality of the hiring process is that oftentimes the person who gets the job was the person who was most well-liked throughout the process. At face value, this seems unfair. But it's actually something you can use to your advantage.

First, it should remind you that you can apply to jobs that may seem out of reach and that you still have a chance. But beyond that, if you are going up against someone who has more qualifications than you, it's your chance to lean into strengths you have beyond hard skills. Highlight ways you work well with others, show your personality, and explain why you'd be a good fit.

Qualifications pique interest, but if the most qualified applicant doesn't fit with company culture, doesn't mesh well with the hiring manager, or has misaligned expectations, they won't get the job.

Myth #4: The Best Time to Ask Questions Is at the End of the Interview

It's common advice to show up to an interview prepared with a few questions to ask. But this doesn't mean you need to sit there like a robot and just answer every question asked of you. An interview is a conversation. Asking questions throughout shows the interviewer that you're engaged and interested, plus it can open up windows to expand the conversation beyond the scripted questions. Prepare your questions in advance and take advantage of the opportunity to ask them as they come up naturally.

Myth #5: The Interviewer Is Looking for Right and Wrong Answers

There is rarely a "right" answer to an interview question, even when there is a case study or project involved. The interviewer wants to see how you think, problem-solve, and approach projects. Focus on storytelling and provide context around why you think a certain way or how you landed on a specific answer.

Ultimately, the best way to differentiate yourself during an interview process is to show up with confidence and be yourself. When you take the pressure off and don't approach the process trying to impress, you can show up as the best version of you. It's a lot easier to put your best foot forward when you're on a level playing field.

Preparing for Each Phase of the Interview

In today's job market, interviewing has become a slog. The process can be long and drawn out, and there are often many more rounds than necessary. Unfortunately, as a candidate you are at the whim of the process, so the best way to get through it is to be prepared.

In a perfect world, the interview process would have only three or four touch points:

- Phone screen
- Hiring manager conversation
- Team interview/panel
- Case study (role-dependent)

Each phase of the interview is different, and how you prepare and show up depends on who you're talking to and what you will be discussing. Regardless of what phase of the interview you are in, the best way to prepare is to create your stories ahead of time. Darci Smith recommends thinking about real-life examples from previous work, volunteer, or educational experience that you can flip to in your head. She refers to this as your "brain Rolodex," meaning that anytime you are asked a question, you can essentially "flip" to an example for your answer.

Let's walk through how to best prepare for each specific interview stage.

Phase 1: The Phone Screen

The phone screen is the first step in the hiring process. It is usually a 15-to 30-minute high-level conversation about your experience. The recruiter will be doing a lot of the talking and sharing more information about the role, the company, and the benefits.

This is your first impression with the recruiter, and it's the company's chance to narrow down the applicant pool. Your first impression with the recruiter is arguably the most important part of the entire process. Not only is it your opportunity to showcase why you should move forward to the next round, but it's also a great time to build rapport. You want the recruiter on your side as they can help advocate for you and your benefits should you get the offer.

How to Prepare

You need to be ready to concisely walk through your resumé. If you move forward with the process, you'll have the opportunity to dive deeper on specific experience with the hiring manager or the team. The phone screen is where you are giving your elevator pitch and telling your story.

The best way to prepare for a phone screen is to anticipate questions you'll be asked and prepare the right questions that you'll ask the recruiter.

Questions to Expect

I've taken probably 100 phone screens, and 99% of the time they all follow the same script:

- *"Tell me about yourself."* This is your elevator pitch. In 60 seconds or less, introduce yourself, share your high-level career journey, an accomplishment, and if you have one, a personal anecdote. This is also a great time to queue up and mention anything on your resumé that you want to focus the conversation on.
- *"Walk me through your resumé."* This is your chance to highlight your career accomplishments, transferable skills, and applicable

experience to the role you're applying for. Make sure you are conscious of time and keep this concise!

- *"Why were you interested in this role?"* You'll want to keep the answer to this question positive. Rather than addressing the concerns or issues with your current role and why you are looking to leave, focus on highlighting the opportunities you see within the role or company you are applying to.

Questions to Ask

The phone screen is just as much a first impression for you as it is for the company. This is your chance to ask your own screening questions to ensure the role is worth pursuing for yourself. Here are a few thought starters:

- *"What is the salary and bonus structure for the role?"* The phone screen is the perfect time to ask about salary and ensure that you are aligned on compensation for a few reasons. First being that salary discussions throughout the interview process happen with HR, not the hiring manager. A phone screen is more often than not with someone in the HR department, so the recruiter should know a range for the position.

  Second, this is where you can qualify whether the opportunity is right before you invest more time and energy into the process. If the range is entirely below what you are looking for, it likely isn't an opportunity worth pursuing. If the role isn't super exciting to you at face value but the compensation is amazing, then you can decide if you'd like to see the process through. Asking about salary isn't taboo and should be discussed up front: at the end of the day, you are at work to be paid!

- *"Why is the last person who left this role leaving?"* Oftentimes, a role exists because someone left. Regardless of the circumstance, the recruiter will most likely answer this question by saying they found a new opportunity. However, this opens the door to some additional information. Sometimes roles exist because of a company reorganization, or because the company is growing and it's a new role that was recently created. This is good information to be aware of as you move throughout the interview process.

- *"What does the remainder of the interview process look like?"* Aligning expectations on the process early on is key. As a candidate, being aware of what to expect, who you will talk to, and the timeline can ease your nerves and make the entire process a lot smoother.

Extra Tips for the Phone Screen

Keep these tips in mind during the phone screen phase as well:

- **Make sure you have a professional voicemail.** This is such an easy thing to do that many candidates overlook. While there is really no reason why a recruiter should hear your voicemail given you will be expecting their call, sometimes it happens. Set up a voicemail that is professional and concise, and double-check that you don't have any old ring back tones lingering.
- **Pay attention to your tone.** Phone screens are difficult because you can't see the other person. It's incredibly important to focus on tone and to make sure you sound upbeat, friendly, and interested. The best way to do this is to talk with a smile and pretend that the other person can see you as you answer questions.
- **Answer the phone professionally.** When the recruiter calls you, don't pick up the phone and say "Hello?" You are expecting their call, and you know who it is. When you pick up, say, "Hi, this is {your name}" with a friendly tone.

Don't let the phone screen intimidate you. It is definitely one of the more important parts of the process, but it is also the most casual.

Phase 2: The Hiring Manager Interview

If you've made it past the phone screen, congratulations! You are now in the selected pool of applicants who will be speaking with the hiring manager and members of the team. Oftentimes, the interview that follows the phone screen is a conversation with the hiring manager.

This is the hiring manager's chance to get to know you, your experience, and what you're looking for. It's another opportunity for a first impression, but this time it's with someone who is intimately involved in the decision-making process, if not the sole decision-maker. Your first impression here is important, so you need to put your best foot forward.

How to Prepare

At this phase, you've already prepared your baseline answers around why you're interested in the role and you should be able to walk through your resumé. For this conversation, you may want to dive deeper into certain areas of your resumé that are specifically related to the role or that highlight transferable skills that would be applicable. It's likely that whatever you mention you will be asked follow-up questions about, so don't speak to anything you aren't comfortable elaborating on.

During this phase, you will be asked behavioral questions. These are questions that ask you to describe an experience or how you'd approach or navigate a certain situation. They are nontechnical storytelling questions, and the main character is you. Oftentimes they start with "Tell me about a time when . . ." or "Give me an example of a situation where . . . ," and they focus on soft skills, such as teamwork, problem-solving, time management, communication, or adaptability.

Luckily, many behavioral questions are easy to anticipate, so you can prepare ahead of time and have your answers ready. Refer back to your "brain Rolodex" and add to it if needed as part of the preparation process.

Here are some behavioral questions to think about:

- *"Tell me about a time when you had to work with someone whose personality was different from yours."* This question is focused on how you communicate and work with people who you don't mesh well with, or how you approach disagreements in the workplace. Ultimately, you want to be honest because disagreements or tension is inevitable, but focus on ending the story with a positive spin.

- *"Tell me about a time where you made a mistake and how you handled it."* This question is pointed at how well you handle being wrong. Mistakes happen, regardless of where you are in your career. This can be an intimidating question because you want to put your best foot forward in an interview. Don't be afraid to be honest and admit a mistake. It shows vulnerability, character, and maturity as well as your ability to learn and improve.

  When I was interviewing, I always used the same answer for this question because there was one very poignant mistake I made that stuck with me. I was communicating with a client via email and was rushed under a deadline. I accidentally addressed the client by the wrong name and immediately realized after I hit Send on the email. My manager—who was cc'd on the note—was not happy and let me know how unprofessional it was in a client-service business.

  However, immediately afterward, I sent a quick one-off note to the recipient apologizing with some light humor. He completely brushed it off and assured me it was no big deal. From that experience, which in hindsight was not a big deal but felt like the end of the world in the moment, I learned two main things: first, pay attention to detail and re-read every email before you send it. I never made that mistake again! And second, humanizing yourself and apologizing goes a long way.

- *"Give me an example of a time where you were under pressure and had to think on your feet."* This is the interviewer's chance to see how you handle working under pressure. In any role, there will inevitably be a time where you're under a deadline, have a full plate, and need to maintain high-quality work. Think about how you work under pressure and the tactics or strategies you implement to stay calm, keep a clear mind, and get things done.

- *"Tell me about a time when an unexpected problem derailed planning. How did you approach it?"* This question is focused on better understanding your time management skills. Basic time management is expected in the workplace, but being able to manage a running to-do list, competing deadlines, and unplanned requests can set you apart from other candidates. Think about the times when you've been the busiest both at work *and* outside of the office, and explain how you balance all of your competing responsibilities. Don't be afraid to give examples outside of the workplace—it shows character and personality. Remember, people hire people.

- *"Describe a time when you were the expert communicating information. What did you do to make sure everyone was able to understand you?"* This is your chance to showcase how you deliver information and can work with others. It's a great opportunity to highlight a presentation you've done, when you've shown leadership qualities, if you've ever presented information to executives, or if you've overseen an intern or other employee.

Convey Your Skills and Experience with Clarity

Smith mentioned the importance of following a framework for answering interview questions. She highlighted the STAR method, which stands for situation, task, action, and result. Following this structure can help you clearly articulate your skill set, experience, and value.

To use this method, think about the following questions:

- What was the **situation** you were going through?
- What was the **task** you were assigned or working on?
- What **action** did you take to accomplish it?
- What was the end **result**? How was it successful?

Utilizing the STAR method makes it easier for the hiring manager to envision you both as an employee and within the open role. It provides insight into your achievements, motivations, and processes that give context to how you operate within the workplace.

The beauty of behavioral questions is that what you talk about is entirely up to you. You control the story, so use this as an opportunity to make yourself shine and highlight your skills.

Extra Tips for the Hiring Manager Conversation

Keep these tips in mind during the hiring manager conversation as well:

- **Prepare for technical questions.** Depending on your line of work, you may get asked technical questions where you need to explain specific concepts or showcase how you use different job-specific software. Ask the recruiter ahead of time if you should be prepared for these types of questions or if the interview will be behavior-based. They will give you some insight on what to expect so you can prepare accordingly.
- **Aim to build personal rapport at the beginning.** Small talk goes a long way. In the beginning of the interview, there is usually a small window of opportunity for some casual conversation. Use this to your advantage, and show your personality.
- **Ask questions about their experience.** People love to talk about themselves, so prepare your questions accordingly. Ask the hiring manager about their specific experience at the company, what they love about the role or team, and how they landed in this position. Not only will it help you learn more about their personality, but it shows that you're interested in getting to know them and value human connection in the hiring process.

The goal of your conversation with the hiring manager is two-fold: highlight your skills and working style while showcasing your personality. The best way to do this is to anticipate questions, have examples prepared, and be yourself.

Phase 3: The Team Interview/Panel

Once you've gained the seal of approval from the hiring manager, you'll have the opportunity to meet other members of the team. While the hiring manager's opinion is important, they will lean on their team to evaluate you as well, both from a cultural fit and a skill fit. It's likely you'll be working with these people more than your hiring manager, so their opinions are important.

How to Prepare

Preparing for a team interview is very similar to preparing for the hiring manager interview. You'll probably be asked some of the same behavioral questions so you can reuse your answers or highlight other examples if you have them. In some cases, you will speak to team members individually, and in others, you'll be faced with a panel.

There are many reasons that a company will use a panel interview to evaluate a candidate:

- To see how you engage with multiple people at once
- To save time in the process
- To gauge additional opinions rather than relying on a sole interviewer

Here are a few tips to ace your panel interview:

- **Do your research in advance.** If you are given the names of the individuals who will be interviewing you, look them up ahead of time. Review their LinkedIn profiles and identify any commonalities. If you know a little bit about them, you can naturally find areas in your conversations to bring it up and build rapport.
- **Maintain eye contact with everyone.** A panel interview is a perfect opportunity for the employer to evaluate your people skills. When answering questions, be sure to look at everyone in the room rather than speaking only to the person who asked the question. Depending on the role of each interviewer, you can also answer questions from their various perspectives.
- **Prepare for follow-up questions.** Panel interviews can lead to additional questions since there are multiple perspectives in the room. Your answer to one question could pique another question from someone else, so be ready to address your replies from different angles. To avoid a scenario where you don't have an answer, be sure to prepare multiple examples for different behavioral questions that could come up.

Panel interviews can be intimidating, but don't let it get to you. Preparation is your best path to success!

Phase 4: The Case Interview

Not every interview process will include a case—and often, the case will come earlier on in the process. That being said, the case interview is usually the biggest hurdle you'll face. This is where the employer is evaluating your hard, technical skills and is also where you are most likely to be asked technical questions.

A *case interview* can be anything from solving a real-life business problem, working through an analysis and presenting your findings, or an example project where you showcase your thought process or creativity. The type of case you are given depends on the role you are applying for, so be sure to research different case types for your industry if you are unsure what to expect.

The purpose of the case interview is for an employer to evaluate the approach you take to problem-solving, how analytical your thinking is, how you use data to quantify and make recommendations, your communication skills, and how you'd approach implementing a solution. It's an opportunity for you to showcase your skills, especially if answering behavioral interview questions isn't your strong suit.

How to Prepare

How you prepare for a case interview largely depends on the case itself, whether it's a take-home case or something you need to do in person, and if you need to prepare and present any materials. Here are some tips to prepare:

- **Research and practice prior case examples.** Many consulting firms have case examples on their websites that candidates can use to practice. These cases are applicable whether you are applying for consulting jobs or other types of roles because they provide examples of questions or prompts that you could be presented with, as well as frameworks to present your answers.

Whether your case interview is in person or prepared at home, take time to work through some practice cases to get used to the questions and ambiguity that you will be presented with. You can search for consulting firms such as Bain & Company, Deloitte, McKinsey, or Boston Consulting Group for case interview examples and preparation tips.

- **Practice presenting out loud.** Case interviews usually require sharing your findings and recommendations in an interview-style setting. You could have amazing answers to the case, but if you don't present them well, it doesn't really matter. Part of their evaluation is how you share and articulate your findings to an audience, so take the time to practice presenting out loud. The key is to do this *out loud*—not in your head. Preparing for a presentation in your head is very different from actually speaking the words and articulating thoughts in a careful and concise way.
- **Don't panic.** Case interviews are by far the most intimidating part of the entire interview process. This is usually the make-or-break part of the interview for many candidates. You are smart enough to work through the case if you've made it to this phase of the interview, so be confident in your abilities. Take a step back, think clearly, and try not to boil the ocean with your answers and approach to the problem.

When it comes to case interview success, practice makes perfect. Even if you don't land the job after your first case interview, it is still excellent practice that you can learn and improve from for your next one. The more you do, the better you'll get and the easier they'll become.

As you progress throughout your career, interviewing will become easier. You'll have more practice, more experience to draw from, and more confidence that you are capable and worthy of landing the jobs you seek.

Key Takeaways

- Interviewing is a two-way street. The interview process is just as much an opportunity for you to evaluate the company as it is for them to evaluate you.
- There are three to four main phases of the interview process: the phone screen, the hiring manager conversation, a team interview/ panel, and depending on the role and company, a case study. Each phase is unique and requires a different strategy and approach to be prepared.
- The best time to talk about money and ensure the salary is aligned with your needs is during the phone screen with HR. Don't make talking about compensation weird—you are at work to get paid!
- To best prepare for conversations with the hiring manager and team, prepare your "brain Rolodex" of behavioral questions and answers that you can use throughout the process. Many behavioral questions focus on how you approach different workplace scenarios such as conflict, problem-solving, and organization or time management.
- Use the STAR method to clearly articulate your experience and skill set during the interview process. This method explains the situation, task to accomplish, action you took, and result.
- When preparing for a case interview, practice out loud. Practicing what you plan to say and articulating your answers verbally is very different and far more beneficial than practicing in your head.

Chapter 5
The Art of Negotiation

In my first job post-grad, it never occurred to me to negotiate my salary. I was just happy to have landed a job that I was moderately excited about! In fact, when I actually received the job offer via email, I was surprised to see so much information regarding 401(k)s, pensions, health insurance, stock options, and more.

It felt like gibberish to me. I remember reading the words and having no idea what they actually meant, what mattered to me, and how to decide what to enroll in. Compensation packages aren't something we are taught in school, and somehow when we finally land a job offer, it's expected that we just know what to do.

My lack of understanding of my compensation resulted in a lag of my earning potential. I knew that I was enrolled in the 401(k), so I selected my percentage and moved on. I was 22 at the time and lucky enough to be able to stay on my parents' insurance plan, so I didn't even bother to look at the insurance options. Beyond the basics, I was offered a pension, which I ignored because I had no idea what that was, and stock options, which I did not exercise because they confused me.

Even writing that out is embarrassing, but unfortunately, it's the norm with young adults who are thrown to the wolves in corporate

America without the necessary tools needed to advocate for themselves and take advantage of the benefits that are offered to them.

As I began the process of finding my second job, my focus was salary and industry. I was desperate to land a very specific job, and I wanted to make more money even though I didn't necessarily have the skill set yet to advocate for it. Ironically enough—as I discussed in Chapter 2—I actually took a pay cut and unknowingly made my first negotiation by requesting a guaranteed bonus.

In this scenario, I didn't evaluate the entire package. I didn't consider work-life balance, the responsibilities of the role, or whether the job would make me happy. I also didn't think about the fact that I was going to be paid monthly rather than biweekly and that the 401(k) was a profit-share that didn't vest until a full year of employment. I didn't make it a full year, meaning that I essentially skipped a year of contributing to my 401(k).

These were mistakes that I could have avoided had I known better. I didn't know enough about total compensation, and I figured as long as I was getting paid equal or more than my prior job, everything was good. I was wrong, and I learned that lesson the hard way.

Throughout this chapter, I break down the nitty-gritty details of compensation packages, including how to evaluate a job offer and negotiation strategies you can implement so you don't make the same mistakes I did. By implementing the lessons you learn, you'll not only feel more empowered to make the right decision throughout your job search, but you'll be able to advocate and negotiate so you are compensated fairly for your skills. Let's dive in!

Compensation Crash Course

There is more to a job than your salary. And I know what you're thinking, because it took me a while to learn that job satisfaction is so much more than your biweekly paycheck.

It's normal to want a high salary at work. Not only is it the most tangible part of your compensation package, but it's also what many of us tie our self-worth to. A *comprehensive compensation package* refers to the total amount of financial and *nonfinancial* benefits that an employee receives from an employer in exchange for their services. It includes various elements that are both direct compensation, such as your salary, and indirect compensation, such as health insurance coverage.

> Evaluating any job opportunity holistically requires looking at the entire compensation package. Understanding what constitutes your total pay can help you determine whether the opportunity is suited to you, or whether there are pillars of the package you want to negotiate.

Compensation packages look different at every company and for every role. Some offer standard base packages that apply to each employee and are then customized based on unique needs or levels at the company. Others are tiered, meaning that total pay, bonus pay, or other factors change as you move upward within the company. Then, there are commission-based packages. These are generally role-dependent and involve both a base salary and commission based on sales or company performance.

Regardless of the type of compensation package you are offered, the goal is the same: to feel incentivized to work and committed to your employer. If you feel you are not being compensated fairly, it's easy to find yourself unmotivated or not care about your work. But if you feel like your company takes care of you, pays you well, and offers you great benefits, you have a reason to perform well so you don't risk losing your job and everything that comes along with it.

While there are other factors that contribute to your overall job satisfaction, such as work-life balance and company culture, your compensation package is very important. There are multiple elements within a comprehensive package that include both direct and indirect pay.

Direct Compensation

Direct compensation is money in your pocket. Think of it as the direct monetary benefit in exchange for your time and work. It can include the following elements:

- **Base salary.** This is a fixed amount of money that your employer agrees to pay you on an annual basis. It's usually paid in fixed increments—weekly, biweekly, or monthly.
- **Hourly wage.** If you don't work a salaried job, an hourly wage is the rate an employee earns per hour of their time. These are common for retail or service jobs, as well as contract opportunities.
- **Bonuses.** Additional pay that an employee may receive based on a variety of factors, including individual or team performance, company performance, or defined parameters within a compensation package. They can be a fixed amount or a percentage of an employee's salary. Many companies today follow a hybrid-tiered bonus structure, where an employee can earn *up to* a defined percentage of their salary depending on a sliding scale of company performance along with individual performance. If the company hits all their targets, the employee can earn a full bonus payout if they have also hit their performance goals. The payout is reduced if the company does not reach its goals or if employee performance is lagging. Bonuses are not only limited to annual performance. Other types of bonuses that could be offered include referrals, holiday, signing, or retention bonuses.
- **Commission.** This is common in sales jobs where an employee's pay is directly connected to their ability to generate revenue. Commission is a percentage of the sales revenue that an employee earns based on their performance.
- **Stock options.** This is a form of equity compensation, meaning the company is giving you equity that you have the right to hold or sell. A stock option is the right to purchase stock at a discounted or predetermined price set by the company. This can be very valuable if the company is high growth.

While this is not an exhaustive list, it covers the majority of the forms of direct compensation. Direct compensation is a critical component of an employee's overall compensation package and can play a significant role in attracting and retaining top talent. Employers often use direct compensation to reward employees for their performance and to motivate them to achieve their goals.

Indirect Compensation

Indirect compensation includes all of the "other" benefits besides what you are actually paid. There are some common examples, such as health insurance coverage or a 401(k), and then there are employee perks that vary depending on the company.

- **Health coverage.** Most companies will offer some type of health insurance for employees to select. Oftentimes, the employer will cover a portion of the monthly premium. In other scenarios, the employer will cover the out-of-pocket premium in its entirety, making it free to the employee. Health coverage can include medical, dental, and vision insurance options for individuals and families.
- **Retirement benefits.** This can include a 401(k) (or a 403(b) if you work at a nonprofit or public company) as well as a company match. A 401(k) is an employer-sponsored retirement plan where the employee can elect to enroll, determine a percentage of their salary to contribute, and have the deduction automatically come out of their paycheck. In certain instances, the employer may provide a match, meaning they will match the employee's contributions up to a certain percentage. This can help accelerate retirement savings. I discuss retirement accounts and matching at length in *Own Your Money* (Allocca 2023).
- **Paid time off.** Also known as vacation time, these are days given to the employee where they can elect to take off while still being compensated. This can include vacation days, sick leave, personal time, or other types of paid leave. Recently, mental

health and "unplug" days have become popular and are commonly included in many new compensation packages.

- **Employee assistance programs.** These are programs that offer counseling, financial, wellness, or other types of services or support for employees. They exist to help employees manage personal and work-related issues.
- **Employee perks.** These can range in size and variety depending on the company. They can include (but are not limited to) access to fitness or gym facilities, meals at the office, transportation allowance, and education or tuition assistance. Famously, companies such as Google provide employees with access to extensive cafeterias and cafés on-site that include free meals and drinks all day, massages, free gym facilities, cooking classes, and top-tier technology.

Indirect compensation can be an incredibly valuable part of a total compensation package. Not only do these types of benefits promote employee well-being, but they can also improve job satisfaction and day-to-day happiness, which is essential for keeping employees motivated and excited about their jobs.

Is Your Compensation Package the Right Fit?

When you have a job offer in hand, you need to evaluate the entire compensation package to determine if it's the right fit for your needs. It's easy to be blinded by a flashy salary and bonus without sufficiently considering the entire situation and the impact it will have on your quality of life today and into the future.

Keep in mind, as you move through different stages of your career, you may value different aspects of your compensation more or less. It's normal to go through phases where making more money is your top priority and you value salary and bonus over PTO and office perks. You will also go through phases where work-life balance and daily quality of life is more important than making as much money as possible. This is okay—it's normal, and it is expected.

Here are a few factors to consider when evaluating a compensation package to determine whether it's the right opportunity for your current situation:

- *Is the direct compensation enough for you to live comfortably?* This is the obvious filter: if the job doesn't pay enough to cover your essential costs and exist without stress, it's a no. If it's the perfect job in every aspect except for the salary, then you may be able to negotiate. I explain some negotiation tactics later in this chapter.
- *Does the indirect compensation cover your needs?* Remember, indirect compensation includes factors such as health insurance, retirement benefits, and PTO. Rank these in order of priority based on what is most important for you and evaluate how the offer stacks up. Most salaried jobs will offer some degree of health coverage and PTO, but not every job offers a retirement plan. Other jobs may offer a lower salary but have very robust indirect compensation such as fully covered health insurance, generous PTO, and 401(k) matching or profit-sharing. Compare your direct and indirect compensation to get the full picture and determine whether it suits your needs at the moment.
- *Are you excited about this job?* It's easy to overlook the realities of a job when a flashy benefits package is right in front of you. Think about what you'll actually be doing and whether it aligns with your personality and skill set. Will you be happy performing the core duties of the job? While money can make any situation a little easier at the beginning, eventually, the higher salary becomes your new normal and the thrill wears off. Think about future you and weigh the pros and cons of your pay with your day-to-day.
- *What will your day-to-day look like?* A new job means your life is going to change. Is the job remote, or will it require you to go into the office each day? If so, what is the commute, and what impact will that have on your availability? Keep in mind that your job can affect your personal life and availability outside of working hours, too, especially if it involves commuting a long distance on a regular basis. Is the compensation worth it? Only you can decide!

- *How will the opportunity bring you closer to reaching your career goals?* I already know this question is annoying, but where do you want to be a year, five years, or even ten years from now? Does this job opportunity provide you with the skills or experience to aid in your career journey? If the job has a robust compensation package but is completely misaligned with the direction you want to take your career, it may be worth reconsidering. Be honest with yourself and your goals.

Your needs and priorities will change throughout your career, so don't look at every job as the be-all and end-all. If it helps, you can create a pro/con list to get the full picture of an opportunity and evaluate whether it suits your needs today and into the future. Ultimately, the only person who can determine whether a job is the right fit for you, is *you*.

Win Your Negotiation

Now that you understand the elements of a compensation package and how to evaluate whether a job opportunity suits you, it's time to learn the art of negotiation.

There will be instances in your job search journey throughout your entire career where you need to negotiate. In fact, *every* job offer should be negotiated so that you are not leaving any money or benefits on the table.

Negotiating a job offer requires both careful preparation and effective communication skills. It truly is an *art*, and you'll get better and more confident the more you do it.

Here is a step-by-step guide on how to negotiate a job offer effectively and successfully:

Step 1: Research and gather relevant information. Understand your market value by researching salaries for similar positions in both your industry and location. You can use resources such as Glassdoor or even LinkedIn, since many states now require companies to publicly post salary ranges for roles.

Don't forget to consider your personal qualifications, experience, perspective, and value you bring to the organization. If you believe you offer something unique, whether it be a strength or a skill, highlight it and use it as leverage during this process.

Step 2: Prioritize your needs and wants. Understanding what aspects of the job offer are most important to you can help you identify where you'd like to negotiate. You *can* negotiate beyond base salary, and if a company isn't able to increase your base, they may be able to provide additional PTO days, a signing bonus, or something else. Identify your must-haves and your nice-to-haves, knowing that you may need to compromise.

Step 3: Plan your strategy. This is your game plan for the conversation. Set clear objectives by defining your target salary range or specific requests you plan to ask for. Use this time as well to consider any objections or concerns from the employer, and have counterarguments prepared to address them. Remember your prioritized needs and wants—if your first request can't be accommodated, be prepared for plan B!

Step 4: Present your case. A negotiation is simply a conversation, so you can schedule time with the recruiter to discuss your offer and present your requests. You need to clearly articulate your value based on your skills, experience, and qualifications to explain why you believe your request for a higher salary or additional benefits is justified. At the end of the conversation the goal is for *both* parties to walk away satisfied, so remember that the goal is to compromise!

Step 5: Let there be silence. After you present your case, respectfully stop talking. Allow the recruiter the space to respond and listen to their perspective. There are three ways it can go: first, they can say no, in which case you decide whether you're willing to accept the offer as is. Second, they can say yes and present you with a counteroffer, and you'll need to decide whether you want to either accept it right then or think about it and circle back. Third, they may say that they need to talk to someone else—this is okay! Oftentimes, there are company policies and budgets that the recruiter doesn't have control over. Let the scenario play out before making a decision.

At the end of the day, negotiation is a conversation that requires compromise, so don't go into it prepared to argue. Maintaining a professional demeanor and positive attitude is one of the best ways to get the result you are looking for.

The Negotiation Sandwich

If you're in a position where you are negotiating a job offer, that means the company already wants you to work for them. It's likely you have a target compensation number in mind, and now it's time to ask for it. Ideally, at the beginning of the interview process you have already aligned with the recruiter on a salary range that you can expect. However, more often than not, the actual offer you receive will be at the lower end of the range. And thus, it's time to implement one of the most effective negotiation strategies out there: the *negotiation sandwich.*

This is both a strategy and a script that you can use when negotiating your job offers throughout your career. It's transferable as well, so you can use it for new offers as well as internal offers if you are being promoted or considering a different role in your current company.

The negotiation sandwich is a framework that "sandwiches" your request between two positive statements.

Step 1 (the Bread)

Start with a positive statement. Thank the recruiter for the opportunity and consideration for the role, and let them know how excited you are. This is also a great time to highlight something you discussed to build rapport.

Example: *Thank you so much for this opportunity! I am so excited about {the role}, {the team}, or {the company} and can't wait to get started!*
Or
Example: *Thank you for this offer! I really enjoyed meeting the team and am excited for this role. It's a great next step for me in my career.*

Step 2 (the Meat/Cheese)

This is where you present the request. Keep in mind, this is a collaborative effort that will require compromise, not a demand. Do not approach this step with a closed question that can be answered with a simple "yes" or "no." It is crucial to provide a number or a range, depending on what aspect of your offer you are negotiating, and keep the request open-ended.

Example: *Based on my skills {highlight one or two skills} and experience doing {provide an example}, as well as the responsibilities discussed throughout this process, I am aiming for a range between X and Y.*
Or
Example: *I would love to accept this offer, but I have a few questions regarding the salary range. Based on my experience with {X, Y, Z}, I am hoping to land within the range of X to Y. Is this a range we can discuss?*

When you present your range, ensure it aligns with previous conversations you have had about salary already, but with a *slight* overshot. For example, if you and the recruiter aligned on a salary range of $70k–$80k during the initial phone screen, and they offered you $70k, a reasonable range to request at this point would be $75k–$80k.

Not only is it unproductive to request a range entirely outside of previously discussed numbers, but it's unprofessional and won't likely result in a successful outcome.

Step 3 (the Condiments)

If you find yourself getting flustered or are met with resistance, this is your opportunity to reiterate that you are hoping to come to an agreement. Condiments are optional, so only add them if you need to or feel it would add to the situation!

Example: *I'd love to work together to find a number/result we can align on!*

Step 4 (the Bread)

Wrap up the conversation with a final gratitude statement. Ending on a high note ensures that the conversation remains positive and highlights that your intentions are to find mutual compromise.

Example: *I am so excited about this opportunity, and I look forward to hearing back. In the meantime, let me know if there is anything you need from me.*

The last step of this process is to stop talking! The most intimidating part of the negotiation is commonly thought to be the ask—but this is incorrect. The most intimidating part of the negotiation is the part where you let the silence sit.

Say your piece, and then don't say anything else. This is where the recruiter will think about the request and respond. Remember, they have already offered you the job; they want you to work there. They will do what they can to accommodate the request within the parameters available.

There may be additional questions that arise, or they may need to regroup with the hiring team to determine the next steps and align on a compromise. Be open to the process, maintain a positive attitude, and let it fall into place.

Strategies for Success

While the negotiation sandwich can provide a helpful framework and script to follow for the actual conversation, negotiation is an ongoing process that begins at the initial phone screen. Here are a few additional tips to keep in mind.

- **Focus on likability.** I touched on this in Chapter 4, but likability is crucial. People will fight for you or stick their neck out for you *if they like you.* Anything you do throughout the interview or negotiation process that makes you less likable can have a direct impact on a successful outcome. Beyond basic manners, focus on building rapport with the recruiter, smile when you talk, and show curiosity. During the negotiation, be receptive to concerns, avoid becoming defensive, and try not to be petty or greedy if the offer is not meeting your standards.

- **Make it clear you are serious.** To get additional approval on salary or other benefits requires effort from the recruiter. You don't know what needs to happen on the other end of the conversation—it could require them to exercise a favor, stick their neck out more than usual, or leverage politics to get you what you want. The likelihood someone will do this for a candidate who is not explicitly serious about accepting an offer is slim. If you are going to negotiate, be clear that if an agreement is reached, you plan to accept the offer.

- **Stay at the table.** Sometimes, you can't get everything you are seeking up front. That doesn't mean that down the line something won't change. Maybe they can't meet you at your highest salary request currently, or they can't approve an additional work from home day at the moment. But, three months down the line, after you've built rapport and generated trust from a few months of working, you can resurface the conversation with a fresh perspective. Be open and willing to revisit, especially when the offer feels right.

Ultimately, finding the right job with the right benefits that you are excited about is *hard*. In most cases, there will be a degree of give-and-take from both parties. It's okay if you need to compromise on something or if there are aspects of the offer that are not absolutely perfect.

Remember that your career will have seasons of high demand, high reward, and slower seasons of work-life-balance and compromise. Maintain perspective, and stay true to your values and needs so that you can find harmony in your role during the season you are currently in!

Key Takeaways

- A compensation package refers to the total amount of financial and nonfinancial benefits that an employee receives from an employer in exchange for their services. Evaluating a job opportunity holistically requires looking at the entire package and weighing the direct and indirect aspects.
- Direct compensation is the monetary benefit awarded to an employee while indirect compensation includes the nonmonetary benefits, such as health insurance, paid time off, or employee perks.
- Successfully negotiating a job offer is an art. To effectively prepare, be sure to research your market value to better understand salaries and compensation packages for similar positions in your industry and location. Plus, keep in mind that you can negotiate beyond your salary and ask for additional PTO days, a signing bonus, or something else.
- The negotiation sandwich is a great strategy to use, ahead of any type of negotiation conversation. You "sandwich" your request between two positive statements. Practice your request out loud—you'll feel more confident when you know exactly what you plan to say.
- When negotiating, don't be afraid of silence. Oftentimes, people think the most intimidating part of a negotiation is the ask, but it's actually the moments after the ask, when you are forced to let the silence sit for a few moments.
- The negotiation starts at the beginning of the interview process. Focus on likability and building rapport. Make it clear you are serious about the role.
- Sometimes you won't be able to get everything you seek during the negotiation. If the job offer is the right fit, stay at the table. You may be able to revisit the conversation at a later date!

Chapter 6
Succeeding
in the Workplace

My corporate career feels like a failure. Not because I struggled to get jobs or because I wasn't smart enough to do the work that was assigned to me. It was because I didn't play the game.

At the time of writing, I've been out of "the game" for a little over a year. I spent five years working a corporate job, three of which I spent also building Break Your Budget on the side. Let's use me as an example here.

If you were to look at me now, you'd view me as successful. I'm 28, I have half a million dollars in the bank, I make multiple six-figures annually, I am self-employed, I've built a thriving business, and I am sitting in my cushy apartment in Los Angeles writing my *second* book.

What you *don't see* is that I never once got promoted in any of my three corporate jobs. The feedback I received in one of my annual performance reviews is that I am not proactive (the irony of this is not lost on me). I've been told I am intimidating, not smart enough, and that I "don't understand financial concepts" (ha!).

I've been passed over for countless jobs, ghosted by recruiters, rejected for not having enough experience and am too embarrassed to admit how many times I have cried at work or in front of colleagues (and even one time, my boss).

Corporate America chewed me up and spit me out. I tried so hard to succeed, from taking professional certifications, going to networking events, pruning my resumé, and biting my tongue in more instances than I can count when I wanted to speak up. I did everything right. Well, *almost* everything. I chose not to play the game, and honestly, I think this is the biggest contributor to why I struggled so much on my corporate journey.

The thing about corporate is that the accolades, the success, the promotion—they don't always go to the person who deserves it most. They often go to the person who correctly plays the game. This is the person who is exceptionally good at kissing ass—which is a skill—or the person who is willing to work extra hours to appease their boss, always be available, and serve as the office punching bag.

Rather than spend an entire chapter of this book teaching you how to fake it till you make it, I'm going to share some practical strategies instead. If I've learned anything in life, it's that the best path to happiness in any area, from personal to professional to financial, is to focus on things you can control.

In a corporate setting, that includes managing your workflow effectively, learning how to advocate for yourself, and identifying situations that can either help or hurt you and then acting accordingly. In this chapter, I teach you how to create a task-management system that can be used to launch your career to new heights without sacrificing your dignity or working 24/7. Let's dive in!

Task Tracking: Why Most People Won't Do It

Despite all of my trials and tribulations throughout my corporate career, there is one thing I consistently did that actually helped me: I tracked my projects and tasks.

It sounds simple, and it is. Over time, I learned the value of task tracking and eventually created my own task-management system that not only helped me stay organized and productive in the workplace but also served as a repository for all the work I was doing that I could refer to during important career moments such as performance reviews and interviews.

Before I get into the good stuff, I'm going to highlight some of the common objections I receive on social media any time I recommend task tracking and maintaining specific details in your workflow to use in the future. I understand that adding steps into your daily workflow and to-do list can feel overwhelming, especially when you already have a full plate. But trust me, your future self will thank you.

TL;DR: Even introducing the idea of task tracking triggers a lot of people. In fact, I have never received more hate and negative comments than I do on my videos related to task tracking and creating this type of system. Before you read the rest of this chapter, if writing down your daily to-do's is going to send you into orbit, go for a walk and pick this back up later.

Okay, let's get into it.

Objection #1: Task Tracking Takes Too Long and Is a Waste of Time

Here are some of the comments I've received on TikTok and Instagram related to the time it takes to track your projects:

> *"I wonder how people have time for this at work. I'm not going to dedicate a ton of precious time to this when there is real work to be done. I jot notes in my planner or my outlook."*

> *"Seems like you're spending a lot of your time just tracking."*

> *"I work in corporate and would never recommend wasting time on this as you lose agility immediately. This sort of behavior brews a culture of failure accountability rather than a culture of celebrating success."*

> *"What a waste of effort and energy. If your organization demands you task track, or you feel so insecure in your employment status that you feel it necessary to task track, work to find another job or work to form a union. This is not worth your effort or time and it is certainly not benefiting your organization."*

Most commonly, people interpret spending any additional time keeping track of your workflow and accomplishments as a waste of time because it (1) takes too long, (2) takes time away from "real work," or (3) requires too much energy or effort. Beyond the actual time commitment of task tracking (hint: it does not take a long time), the other argument related to this objection is that if your company wants to lay you off or fire you, having a list of your accomplishments won't make a difference, and it's of no benefit to your employer.

What these objectors are missing is twofold:

- **The goal of creating a task-management system isn't to avoid or fight against being laid off.** It's also not to benefit your employer. If your company is going through layoffs, you can't control your fate. The purpose of creating a task-management system is to have a running list of your projects and accomplishments to leverage if and when *you* choose to change jobs or ask for a promotion, which as we've discussed in previous chapters is very important to have on hand (remember the "brain Rolodex"?) Plus, if you do find yourself laid off, at least you have a repository of what you accomplished in your prior role that you can use to kick-start the job-hunting process with confidence.
- **The maintenance needed to manage a task-management system isn't time-intensive if you are consistent with it.** As you read through this chapter, you may start to wonder, "Where will I find the time in my day to do all of this?" Surprise! You already have the time in your day to do it. Plus, you don't really need a ton of time; you need about 10 minutes per day.

Not having time isn't an excuse—there is not a single person out there who is working a full eight-plus-hour day in a corporate job without taking a single break between the hours of 9 a.m. and 5 p.m. to look at their phone. You have the time; you're just choosing not to use it on things that can actually help you.

Objection #2: Task Tracking Is a Form of Micromanagement and Means Your Workplace Is Toxic

"I work in corporate, have an awesome company, but this reminds me of prior work, micromanagement . . . toxic. Keeping a log or 'task tracking' is micro management."

"Any place where you feel you must justify every part of your day to prove you add value or as proof you deserve a raise/promotion IS NOT where you need to be. Move on now before the toxicity seeps into your attitude and drive. #beentheredonethatgotthetshirt"

"This is like having a meeting about having a meeting about having another meeting."

It's the #beentheredonethatgotthetshirt for me. Just kidding. Let's unpack this one, because it's a doozy.

Many workplaces—toxic ones included—require employees to submit timesheets or time logs to ensure that they are actually doing their job and not wasting time on the company's dollar. It's also a very common practice in consulting or client-based roles because employees need to submit their "billable hours" so the company can be paid for project-based work.

To be clear—this is totally fair for a company to do. They hire you and pay you to work, and it's their prerogative to ensure that you are actually working during the time you're getting paid.

It's usually the way these timesheets are implemented or scrutinized by management that leads to this toxic belief. Because of this, I can understand why so many people believe that a detailed task-management system can be interpreted as toxic behavior or a form of micromanagement.

However, these objections are completely missing the point.

The purpose of task tracking and ultimately a task-management system that highlights your value-add and accomplishments isn't to prove to the company that you are worthy. The purpose is *for you* to have all of the information you need to advocate and stick up for yourself during important career moments.

For example, let's say that you are up for a promotion in your end-of-year review, and it's contingent on reaching a specific set of goals. You get into your meeting, and your manager says, "Sorry, you didn't accomplish X, Y, Z, so you'll have to wait until next year for the promotion."

But wait—you *did* accomplish X, Y, *and* Z! And guess what. With the proper record, you can bring that up in the meeting right then and there, show your manager that you did in fact accomplish your goals, and advocate for the promotion you both earned and deserve. You can do this with confidence, because you have the proof and are prepared to talk about it.

Imagine you don't have that record ready to go. *You* know you did it, but there's no proof. And then guess what. You're flustered, upset, and hastily digging through your email, calendar, and desktop for proof that your goal was met when your manager seems to think otherwise. Guess who didn't get the promotion.

That's just a simple example—but it highlights how important it is to have your accomplishments ready. You do so much at work, and so does your manager. You are both bound to forget a lot of the work you've done, especially if you work in a fast-paced environment where priorities and projects are changing all the time.

The biggest lie you tell yourself is: "I don't need to write that down. I'll remember it."

Objection #3: If You Have a Good Manager, They Will Do It For You

> *"If you have a good manager, they will set up regular meetings with you to discuss what you're working on and what you need."*

> *"Mid-level women in business . . . do you think your boss does this? But you keep doing you."*

> *"If you have to track every task, it means you don't have the right boss. If your boss has juice and likes you, you're gonna get raises and promotions."*

This one sends *me* into orbit. It is not your manager's responsibility to keep track of your work! It's yours.

It's common thought that a "good" manager is consistently giving you great work, keeping track of your accomplishments, seeing how awesome you are, encouraging you to learn, and advocating for you at every possible instance.

When have you ever had a manager like that? Most managers suck—that is the hard truth. In fact, it's easy to forget that on top of managing you, your manager also has a job to do and they are relying on you to do your job so they don't have to worry about it. Everyone in the workplace is selfish and looking out for their own best interest first—don't assume otherwise.

> Your manager—good or bad—is not keeping track of your accomplishments. Sure, they are likely keeping a pulse check on what you have going on and making sure that you are getting your work done. But they're only doing that so *they* look good to *their* manager. And most likely, they aren't spending very much time on it unless you are causing an issue.

Your job is *your* career. In my effort to help you own your career, it's my job to give you the tough love: if you don't own your career, no one will. Your manager's job is to help guide you in your role, whether it be teaching you a process, overseeing a project that you are on, maybe providing you with a learning opportunity or advocating for you here and there. And that's if you have a good one; remember, most are not good. Most managers are paying attention to their own stuff and are really just making sure that you don't get in the way of that.

If you think that your manager is going to keep track of your work and just "remember" everything you've done when the important conversations happen, you are sorely mistaken. You are going to be very disappointed when those meetings come around and you leave them the same way you went in.

You and only *you* are your best advocate at work. Don't rely on anyone else to do it for you, even if you have the best manager ever.

Building Your Task-Management System

With the hard part out of the way, it's time to learn the basics of effective task management. There are four key elements to my task-management system that I still carry with me today on my self-employment journey.

Setting Annual Career Goals

The first element is setting annual career goals. There are three types of career goals that I set.

- **Role- or project-related goals.** These goals are directly related to your job description and the responsibilities of your role. It's likely that your manager has some role-related goals for you already and they ladder up to both team and company-wide goals. If your manager does not have any goals in mind, you can still set your own. Think about the core responsibilities of your job and what you are hired to do. How does your job contribute to the broader company goals? What do you need to accomplish in your role to be successful?
- **Development goals.** These are goals related to developing new skills or honing a current skill set. Think about the skills you want to learn or the areas of your role and/or career you enjoy that you want to lean into.
- **Income goals.** These are goals related to increasing your income, both inside and outside of the workplace. They can be related to getting a raise or a promotion at work or even starting a side hustle or a business.

Goal setting is an excellent way to set clear directions on how you plan to navigate your career. In order to actually implement your goals, you need to define the parameters, important metrics, and action steps needed to reach them. For each goal you set, define the following:

- **Priority and size of goal.** You can either rank your goals in order of priority or assign them a level, such as high, medium, or low. Evaluating the size of the goal, and subsequently all the tasks or projects that fall below it, can aid in determining how to prioritize and where to focus your time.

- **Deadline.** Determining a deadline can help with prioritization, but also with mapping out your year and creating a plan for accomplishing the goal.
- **Measurable output.** This is your success criteria for accomplishing the goal. How will you measure your progress and output related to it?
- **Stakeholder.** If the goal is role- or project-related, it's likely there is an internal stakeholder who benefits from the goal being accomplished. Identify who the relevant stakeholders are so you can lean on them or turn to them for questions as you work through it.
- **Value-add or skill developed.** Every goal you are working toward has impact and value in the workplace. What is the impact of the goal, and how does it add value at work and within your own professional development? Identifying this ensures that what you are working toward benefits both you and your employer.

> At the beginning of each year, I recommend setting up to three goals of each type and reevaluating them every quarter.

Tracking Your Tasks

The second element of your task-management system is actually tracking the tasks on a regular basis. However, a successful system goes beyond a simple weekly to-do list. You can track the value-add of each task or project, follow-ups, stakeholders you are working with, feedback you receive, unplanned requests, and accomplishments.

- **To-do list.** At the start of each week, create a to-do list for all the work you need to get done with a focus on higher-level projects or tasks. Be sure to note deadlines or due dates as needed, as well as any important meetings and preparation necessary. I know this sounds super basic, but creating a thorough to-do list sets the structure for your entire week and helps ensure you aren't wasting your time.

- **Value-add.** For each project or task included on your weekly to-do list, aim to identify the *value-add*. This could be a skill you are learning as a result of working on the project, a process that you are improving, how you are enabling someone else to do their job—the list is endless. Think about the impact the work has on you, the people you work with, and the company.

> Identifying the value-add for your tasks is essential for a few reasons. First, if you struggle to find any value for the majority of work you are doing, it may be a good time to seek additional responsibilities or search for a new job. Second, it highlights the impact of the work you do and the skills you are developing, which can be leveraged when you are advocating for yourself throughout your career.

- **Follow-ups.** Throughout your workweek, you are attending meetings, messaging with colleagues, and receiving emails that require a response. Keeping track of follow-ups from these events will make it easier for you to stay organized and enable you to be proactive on the job. Plus, follow-ups often create work that adds value, which you can add to your running list.
- **Unplanned requests.** The bane of my existence in the workplace was always the "Hey Michela, do you have a minute?" message. This meant someone needed me to do them a favor or something was going to be added to my plate. It's to be expected that during the week you will get unplanned requests as new information comes to light or priorities change. Keep track of these, along with who requests them, as you can leverage them later to request feedback.

- **Accomplishments.** At the end of each week, spend 10 minutes reviewing your weekly project log and highlight two to five of your biggest accomplishments. Did you complete any projects, present in a meeting, identify a bottleneck, come up with a solution to something, or simply accomplish everything on your list? Write it down, because you can leverage this information when updating your resumé, interviewing, or advocating for yourself during important conversations. Be sure to also note if any of these accomplishments directly ladder up to either progress toward or completing one of your annual goals.

I know that this sounds like a lot to keep track of every week, and you're probably wondering where you'll find the time to maintain such a detailed log while also doing your job—cue the *"Who has time for this?!"* objection. Luckily, keeping up with task tracking at this level is actually quite easy and can be done in less than 10 minutes per day.

You can take five minutes in the morning to review your to-do list and create your game plan. You're likely already doing this in some capacity, so by creating a system you can formalize it so it works even better for you long-term. If any new requests have come up, you can add them to your log, and then go about your workday as scheduled. At the end of the day, spend five minutes reviewing what you worked on and writing down any additional details you deem necessary.

This five-minute wrap-up at the end of the day is called a *shutdown routine*, and it's a tactic I learned when reading the book *Deep Work* by Cal Newport (2016). Essentially, a shutdown routine is where you close the current workday, plan out the next day, and then quite literally shut down your work and focus on your personal life. Before you log off, take five minutes to write your final notes, scan your list for tomorrow's tasks, and then disconnect from work and utilize your free time to enrich your life. By incorporating a shutdown routine, you can ensure that you don't forget any tasks that you weren't able to complete while also making the mental switch from work to personal.

Implementing a Monthly Reflection

The third level of your task-management system at work is implementing a monthly reflection. In *Own Your Money*, I discuss how to complete a monthly money review and how there are so many benefits to consistently reviewing how you are using and approaching your money, self-reflecting on what is and isn't working, and then making tactical adjustments to continuously improve. This same process can apply to your career and be incredibly valuable.

- **Highlight your top three to five accomplishments from the month.** Look back at your weekly task logs and identify the most important accomplishments. From there, aim to align each accomplishment with an annual career goal to ensure that you are actually making progress toward the goals you set.
- **Collect any feedback you received.** Feedback is essential, whether it's positive or constructive. You can leverage positive feedback as supporting evidence during performance reviews, and you can utilize constructive feedback to highlight how you have addressed the issue and implemented changes as a result. I recommend keeping some sort of folder on your desktop and adding any feedback you receive to it all month long, no matter how big or small.
- **Set two to three goals for the next month.** Goal setting provides direction, so if you are working on any larger projects or receive feedback that you need to address, be sure to incorporate it into your goals. You can review and assess the goals each month and ensure they ladder up to the annual goals you set.

Creating a Promotion Plan

The final phase of your task-management system is your promotion plan. This is definitely optional but very helpful if you are hoping to be promoted or make any sort of movement in your career. Here is how to create a promotion plan:

- **Identify the core responsibilities of the position you seek.** It is critical to understand what would be expected of you in the role you'd like to be promoted into. You can easily find this information within a job posting description, so look on your internal job site or ask your manager or the HR department for the information. You can also look at similar job postings externally. Beneath each core responsibility, identify the high-level actions you would take in that role to satisfy those responsibilities.
- **Highlight examples of aligned work you've already done.** What have you done in your current job already that is aligned to the role you seek? Think about transferable skills and how they can apply to various roles at different levels or across different industries.
- **Identify the gaps.** Obviously if you are looking to be promoted into a role that is different from the role you are in, whether it be a level up or a lateral move into a different industry, there are going to be experience gaps that need to be filled. This is why it's so important to understand the core responsibilities of the role you seek as well as the work you've already done that may be aligned. Some of these gaps will be filled directly on the job, but some of them can be filled in your current role either through development projects or additional responsibility that you can request. Being aware of these gaps is key so you can start working toward filling them.

To summarize, a task-management system consists of setting annual career goals, tracking your tasks and accomplishments weekly, implementing a monthly career review, and creating a promotion plan. It sounds like a *ton* of work, but in practice it should only take a few minutes per day to maintain and about 30 minutes per month to work through a review. I maintain my own task-management system using the *Own Your Career Template,* which is available at www.breakyourbudget.com/shop.

The Benefits of Using a Task-Management System

There are innumerable benefits to implementing this type of system, but here are a few of the most important:

- **Highlight the work you actually enjoy.** It's likely that there are parts of your job that you like and parts of your job that you dislike. When you keep track of what you are working on, you can identify how much of your workload is dedicated toward things you enjoy doing and how much is being spent on things you dislike. If the proportions are totally off, then you know it may be time to make a change. You can also leverage this to seek out different opportunities aligned with your interests.
- **Remember the work you do.** You do *so much more* at work than you realize. If you don't keep track of it, you can't leverage it in the future. What gets recorded, gets managed.
- **Advocate for yourself.** I've mentioned this a few times throughout this chapter so far, but having a running list of not only the projects you are working on but also the value you add, the feedback you receive, and your accomplishments can help you during important moments in your career. You can leverage this information to advocate for why you deserve a raise or a promotion, to update your resumé, or to use as part of your running "brain Rolodex" for interviews as mentioned in previous chapters.

> Remember, you are your own best advocate at work, and a great way to build confidence in the workplace is to draw awareness to just how valuable you are.

Don't look at a task-management system as something that benefits the company or your manager—view it as a tool that benefits *you*. It may not protect you from getting laid off, but it *will* put you in the driver's seat of your career.

Executive Career Profiles

While my best advice for succeeding in the workplace is to focus on the areas of your career that you can control, my perspective is just one of many. And so, to conclude this chapter, I am highlighting career advice from seasoned professionals—those who have been in the corporate arena for a long time, have adapted to the new age of working, and who have climbed the ladder—or built their own— with success.

I interviewed five tenured professionals who have forged successful careers for themselves over the last 40 years. These are executives, leaders, and entrepreneurs who have navigated various career paths and learned countless lessons along the way.

Paul Maier

Title: Principal, 9th Avenue Advisory Services LLC
Industry: Collaboration and IT/Cloud Services
Bio: Paul Maier is a retired business executive with over 40 years of experience. He has held leadership positions in client services, enterprise sales, product management, cloud transformation, and M&A (mergers and acquisitions). In addition to leading and growing businesses, he has led multiple accretive M&A processes and integrations and played an active role in multiple liquidity events. He is also a certified executive coach (PBCA). Paul has extensive experience in all aspects of collaboration and customer solutions and services, as well as all aspects of portfolio development and professional and managed services optimization. He holds an MBA from Fairleigh Dickinson University and has

attended an international graduate school in France. He is also a university guest lecturer for an Executive and Entrepreneurial MBA program.

What are some of the most important lessons you've learned from your career?

- You can learn from everybody, and you should treat everybody with dignity and respect, regardless of what level they are. If you can build a relationship, and people know that you truly care about them, they will trust you and partner with you to achieve your shared objectives.
- Be open to input and take up new ideas. Don't be the person who says, "We've tried that before; it didn't work." Think about how you can start with "yes" instead of with "no." This will help engage people and get them comfortable talking about their ideas so you can collaborate and work toward a solution or a goal.
- When working with customers or stakeholders, be inquisitive. Don't be a salesperson—be a businessperson. Take the time to understand what they are trying to achieve, how you can measure success, and how they measure progress. Be as quantitative as possible.
- Don't confuse motion and progress. You need to focus on what you are trying to achieve versus being busy. Follow the KSS model: Keep doing these, Stop doing these, Start doing these. Use this to structure your day and audit your time so you are focusing on what is most important to you and your prioritized objectives.

When working with young professionals, what do you look for in someone who you believe will be successful in their career?

- Energy, curiosity, and work ethic.
- They are influential and active in their social network in the workplace. For example, they could be a really smart technical person or a really charismatic marketing person who has the ability to influence their peers and have the emotional intelligence to lead.

- They have grit. They are willing to double down when things get hard and aren't going to run away from a problem.
- They are a team player. It sounds cliché, but the name on the front of the jersey is a lot more important than the name on the back.

If you could go back to your 20s, what career advice would you give to your younger self?

- Write down what you've accomplished and be as quantitative and detailed as possible. When you're writing a resumé, don't talk about actions—talk about results and impact.
- Be a student of the game, read business books, talk to business people, and continuously invest in yourself. Most people don't want to hear it, but life is a competition, and it's a heck of a lot more fun when you win! To win, you have to prepare, plan, practice, and learn. Game on!

Kathy Doherty

Title: Executive Vice President, Merchandising at Fortune 500 Company
Industry: Retail
Bio: Kathy Doherty has over 35 years of experience working her way through a Fortune 500 company in the retail industry. She started her career as a buyer and over time was promoted into various management positions, ultimately becoming an executive vice president at a billion-dollar company. Kathy also runs a women's leadership group that helps women of all ages and levels in the company navigate the workplace throughout different phases of life to ensure they are reaching their fullest potential.

What are some of the most important lessons you've learned from your career?

- Focus on finding something you love about your work. Whether it be the company you work for or the industry you work in, it's a lot easier to be successful when you enjoy what you are doing every day.

- Look for a company that has integrity, values you align with, and is willing to invest in your development and talent as an employee. If a company isn't willing to invest in you, it may be a sign to find other opportunities.
- The definition of career success is internal. What do you view as success? Stay true to yourself and don't let external factors influence your decisions, because ultimately you are the one showing up to that job every day.
- Listen to other people to learn. When someone isn't great at what they're doing, they often don't listen to why. If you receive constructive criticism or feedback, take the time to really understand why and what you could have done differently. Be comfortable looking in the mirror and asking for feedback so you can grow.

When working with young professionals, what do you look for in someone who you believe will be successful in their career?

- Someone who is good and kind. In most corporate jobs, you aren't curing cancer—so being a genuine person who works hard, is flexible, curious, and is passionate about something will take you far.
- Softer qualities are the most important, especially for developing culture at a company. You can be taught business and technical skills, and you don't have to be the smartest person in the room, but who you are, the perspective you have, and the obstacles or challenges you've faced make you stand out.

If you could go back to your 20s, what career advice would you give to your younger self?

- Stop worrying so much! So many people worry about what people think of or say about them, but in reality, they are not worried about you—they're worried about themselves.

- Don't be afraid to make mistakes, try more things, take more risks, and believe in yourself more.
- Support each other. Especially if you are a woman, support other women. Never be a part of bringing someone down, and don't be afraid to bring someone up and highlight their success.

Frank Flynn

Title: President, National Electronics Company
Industry: Electronics
Bio: Frank Flynn has over 40 years of experience working in corporate development and mergers and acquisitions within the electronics industry. He has spent nearly half of his career serving as the president of his current company, where he also served as COO, CFO, and director of corporate development. Throughout his career, he has led the execution of the company's strategic growth plans, doubling the size of the company and growing the business to nearly half a billion dollars. Frank holds a BA in economics from Harvard University and an MBA in finance and marketing from UCLA's Anderson School of Management.

What are some of the most important lessons you've learned from your career?

- Don't be afraid to consider your happiness above the money. Think about what is driving you and motivating you to pursue your career.
- If something in your career isn't working, take the foundations of what you have learned in school and at work and translate it to other areas. There is great disparity between what people want to do and what provides a good income base, but within this disparity there is opportunity to leverage your experience into something else.
- Your goal should be to pursue something with a combination of happiness, monetary benefit, and socialization. Socialization is incredibly important. Prioritize your life outside of work. Meet people and build your life, not just your career.

When working with young professionals, what do you look for in someone who you believe will be successful in their career?

- Technical skills matter a lot less than your drive and competitiveness. I want to see someone with drive because I can teach them the technical skills while molding them into a leader.
- Most people are not committed and are always looking for the next opportunity too fast. If you don't want to be somewhere, then it's fine to leave. But if you are in a good situation, give it enough time to develop and gain experience instead of constantly searching for the next best opportunity to make more money.

If you could go back to your 20s, what career advice would you give to your younger self?

- Take more time to understand the opportunities that exist and where they can take you. Talk to more people, get more perspective, and evaluate how an opportunity can shape your career beyond the immediate term. The decision you're making may not necessarily be one for the long term, but think about what you are trying to build on and let it take shape over time.
- Remember, things are going to go right, and things are going to go wrong, so you have to learn how to adjust and adapt and be comfortable making changes.

Lisa Allocca

Title: Cofounder and CEO, Red Javelin Communications
Industry: Public Relations, Digital Marketing, Technology
Bio: Lisa Allocca is an entrepreneur with over 35 years of experience in global marketing, public relations, product management, market strategy, and industry analysis. Having spent half of her career as a client and the other half operating an agency, she has developed a unique perspective of the challenges businesses face and how

to strategically position companies to rise to leadership positions. Lisa is active in collegiate-level entrepreneurship programs and is a three-time guest lecturer at MIT Sloan School of Management. (She is also my mom!)

What are some of the most important lessons you've learned from your career?

- After spending the first half of my career in corporate and the second half as an entrepreneur, I've found that success in a corporate job looks very different from success on your own. Corporate is all about group decision-making, fostering processes around decision-making, and aligning teams, while entrepreneurship requires outward focus, agility, and flexibility. Learn how to lean into your environment and develop the skills that will make it possible for you to thrive both where you are and where you want to be.
- If you want to thrive as an entrepreneur, you can't beat every decision to death. You are making fast decisions every day, and you don't always have the resources to analyze everything. Learn how to refine as you go, and be comfortable taking risks and letting scenarios play out. My company started as a PR firm in the early 2000s, but as the digital age has evolved, we have had to be adaptable and reinvent ourselves to align with current times.

When working with young professionals, what do you look for in someone who you believe will be successful in their career?

- Someone who is smarter than me and can challenge me at every step. They are the people who want to get their hands dirty and are willing to do the work so they can learn.
- The most important personality trait is grit. Someone who can think on their feet and doesn't let it go. If there's a problem to be solved, they're going to figure out how to solve that problem, even if it seems impossible. I can outsource technical skills, but I can't teach someone to want to be there.

If you could go back to your 20s, what career advice would you give to your younger self?

- Find a better balance in your life. When I started my career, hard work and long hours typically paid off, but you paid a huge price in your personal life. I got a later start than I wanted to in my personal life because of that. Be sure to balance your life from day one, as much as you possibly can.

Timothy Duffy

Title: CEO of TD Enterprises
Industry: Military, Professional Services
Bio: Tim Duffy is the president and CEO of TD Enterprises and a retired colonel in the Air Force Reserves. He has 30 years of military experience, including roles as a US Air Force Officer, Decorated Combat Fighter Pilot, Director of Operations (Massachusetts Air National Guard), and Colonel/Regional Reserve Director (US Air Force Reserves). He is also a pilot with United Airlines. Duffy simultaneously translated his military excellence toward a career in leadership development and strategic business consulting, where he advises some of the largest Fortune 100 companies in the world. He also developed the Innovative Advanced Leadership Program (ALP) to develop talent and grow leadership across all levels of an organization.

What are some of the most important lessons you've learned from your career?

- Be focused and have specific, measurable, and time-bound goals. Often people set goals and don't have success criteria in place to measure progress and reach them. But without that information, you can't go back and understand the process, regardless of whether you reached the goal or not. You need to understand what went well so you can replicate it going forward, what didn't go well so you can adjust in the future, and whether there were external factors at play.

- Aim to stay unemotional when making decisions. Even if you don't have specific job knowledge, learn how to make decisions under pressure and don't let emotions cloud your judgment. People will use certain words or phrases to generate an emotional response, such as "emergency," "all hands on deck," and "crisis." Learn to recognize them for what they are and don't let them get you emotional. As you move throughout your career, you get paid for the quality of your decisions, especially if you are in a position where your decisions effect change.
- Hold yourself to a high standard and don't be afraid of honest feedback.

When working with young professionals, what do you look for in someone who you believe will be successful in their career?

- People with a positive outlook and a can-do attitude. I would prefer to work with someone who has less talent and a great attitude versus someone with more talent and a bad attitude.
- Seek out experience and listen. A lot of folks who are really smart don't listen. They ask questions, but they're already trying to figure out the next step without listening to the answer. You can gain experience from other people by listening to other people's experiences and stories.
- Look at other people's hesitation as an opportunity. The workplace is starving for leaders, so use that as your opportunity to step up and learn.

If you could go back to your 20s, what career advice would you give to your younger self?

- You're accountable for your decisions. When you make a good decision, everyone celebrates with you. When you make a bad decision, you own it all by yourself. Making a hard call is hard—but it's an opportunity to be a leader.

Key Takeaways

- The unfortunate truth of corporate America is that oftentimes the promotions, success, and accolades don't go to the smartest or most qualified person in the room—they go to the person who knows how to play "the game." The best thing you can do is learn how to effectively advocate for yourself and focus on the things you can control.
- You are your own best advocate. A great strategy to manage your workflow and put yourself in the driver's seat of your career is to create a task-management system.
- Task tracking in the workplace is not micromanagement. It is your responsibility to keep track of what you're working on and your accomplishments so you can better advocate for yourself during career conversations. The purpose of doing it is not to benefit your employer—it's to benefit you!
- There are four key elements to a task-management system: setting annual career goals, tracking your tasks, implementing a monthly reflection, and creating a promotion plan.
- It takes 10 minutes per day to maintain your system. Spend five minutes in the morning outlining your to-do list, and five minutes at the end of the workday working through a shutdown routine that closes out the current workday and sets the tone for the next day.

Chapter 7

Increasing Your Income

You've officially reached my favorite part of this book: the side hustle–to-business pipeline. It's pretty safe to say that I would not be writing this if I had never taken the leap and started a side hustle. My side hustle changed my life and yours can, too. In 2019, I started Break Your Budget on Instagram. I spent the first few months of this new endeavor sharing my best personal finance tips, largely consisting of lessons and takeaways I was learning from my corporate job and in real life. I was working in the investment and finance industry so I learned a lot about the stock market, investing, and how to manage your money.

It was also the same time that I was working the job where I took a pay cut, so I was navigating the challenge of allocating my income, optimizing my budget, and saving, which I was candidly sharing on my Instagram as well. I wasn't necessarily struggling financially, but I was in a position where I was itching to make more money. I recognized Break Your Budget as a potential avenue to do so, and I began taking one-on-one budgeting clients where I'd help them build a budget and learn the basics of personal finance.

My social media journey was a slow roll—after about one year, I reached 1,000 followers on Instagram. This was at the height of the pandemic, so everyone was still at home, the economy was in turmoil, and the need for financial education and awareness was at its peak. I decided to take advantage of this time to lean into educating. I shared tips for navigating recessions, what to do with your finances when you get laid off, and how to stay mentally strong during stock market fluctuations.

In the summer of 2020, I created the *Personal Finance Dashboard (PFD)*, which is my now signature financial planning tool. It was born from both my own desire to have a budgeting spreadsheet that functioned in a way that suited my personal needs, as well as from the need to provide a tool to implement the teachings from my one-on-one budgeting consults for my clients.

Luckily, I used Excel every day at work, so I was able to leverage that skill to build this comprehensive spreadsheet to manage and track my money. I was working toward reaching a six-figure net worth and was saving for a condo, so I was obsessive over my spending and saving and wanted a tool that would give me actionable insight to continue to improve my position. Adding the PFD to my business helped me generate some extra income in addition to my budgeting clients, but it was when I got onto TikTok that everything changed.

TikTok in 2020 was very different from what it is today. I'd consider 2020 and even 2021 the "Golden Age" of TikTok, because the culture on the app was really casual, the videos didn't need to be high-production, and it wasn't super hard to go viral and gain a following. I started posting on TikTok at just the right time: I was one of the first female finance creators on the app, and I gained 100,000 followers in less than a month.

Posting on TikTok is what turned Break Your Budget from a side hobby to a full-blown business that could actually turn into a real job. At the beginning of 2021, I started working with brands, my Instagram following started to grow, I was getting better at creating content, and I started selling a lot more templates without a lot of additional effort.

A couple of months later, I moved to Los Angeles. Now I know what you're thinking: *a white girl who wants to be an influencer gets her 15 minutes of social media clout and moves to LA to pursue her dreams.* LOL. Let me stop you right there: I didn't move to California with the intention of working for myself. I moved out here to enrich my life—I had been living at my parents' house for 16 months since the pandemic started, and I desperately needed a change.

I was lucky that my job allowed me to continue working remotely from Los Angeles, and I used the time outside of my nine-to-five to focus on Break Your Budget, continue working with brands, build my network, and lean into the creator culture that this city offers. After about six months, I reached a precipice: I was passed over for a promotion at work, and I was making over six figures with my side hustle, which was more than my corporate job.

Rather than clawing my way for a promotion that I was already overqualified for, I decided to quit my job and dive into Break Your Budget full-time. I have never once looked back and, to this day, it still stands as the best decision I have ever made.

My life has done a complete 180 since leaving my corporate job: I've written two books, I quadrupled my annual income, and I've built a thriving business that allows me to live my life on my own terms.

I am not special. You can do this, too. In this chapter, I share with you everything you need to know about starting and scaling a six-figure side hustle. If you've gotten this far and are just *tired* of the corporate game, you're going to love this. Buckle up, because it's going to be a long one!

Side Hustles 101

Side hustling has become quite the buzz over the last few years. I think it's because Gen Z has realized the realities of a lifetime working a corporate job: you don't have control over your time or life, and being underpaid in exchange for more than 40 hours of your week for 45 years straight sort of . . . sucks.

Plus, we now live in a world with democratized access to the Internet via a smartphone. There are social media apps that make building an audience, growing a business, and advertising not only accessible to the masses, but *entirely free*.

In fact, in the span of two years selling digital templates, I've made over $500,000 in template and course revenue *without ever running a paid ad.* To see those types of numbers before social media existed, you would need to spend thousands of dollars for advertisements and exposure. Now, you can spend virtually nothing and leverage organic traffic to funnel leads and customers to your business.

I share this to illustrate how accessible side hustling has become, and how regular people like me are utilizing the free tools available to increase their income and change their lives. Anyone can start a side hustle and begin earning extra income; but even with this information, most people won't.

There are two types of side hustles you can choose from:

- **Skill-based side hustle.** This is a side hustle that leverages a specific skill, expertise, or specified knowledge to generate income. It involves utilizing your skills—or learning a new skill—to provide products, services, or solutions for other people. The beauty of a skill-based side hustle is that you can monetize your abilities and passions while providing value to other people. It's a win-win!
- **Low/no skill side hustle.** This type of side hustle does not require you to monetize a specific skill. To be clear, adopting this type of side hustle does not mean that it doesn't require *any* skills or that if you pursue this option, you have no skills. They are the types of gigs that you can get from leveraging a third-party app, dedicating a few hours each day, and earning cash pretty quickly. Think driving for Uber, shopping on Instacart, or walking dogs on Rover.

Before I share how to choose your side hustle, let's break down the pros and cons of each type.

Skill-Based Side Hustles

Break Your Budget is a skill-based side hustle. I had an interest that I was inherently passionate about (personal finance), and I monetized it by leveraging a preexisting skill set (creating Excel templates). I took it a step further by learning new skills like copywriting, social media selling, video editing, podcasting, and more to monetize in other ways. I didn't know anything about these crafts before starting Break Your Budget, but I took the time to learn and develop these skill sets so I could continue to grow my business.

Every person reading this book has a skill to monetize, even if you don't think you do. And if for some reason you can't think of *anything*, there is a skill out there for you to learn. But before you determine if a skill-based side hustle is the way to go, it's important to understand how much time, effort, and work goes into getting it off the ground.

Pros of a skill-based side hustle:

- **Leverages your interests to learn.** The best part of a skill-based side hustle is that you can lean into your own personal interests. This makes it feel less like "work" and more like a passion project. Beyond leaning into your current interests, you can also learn new skills that you may not be able to learn on the job.

  In my own experience, I have always been super passionate about personal finance, but I also felt like I couldn't exercise the creative part of my brain at work. I used Break Your Budget as an outlet for sharing my passions and as an avenue to learn more about my other areas of interest, such as marketing and social media. This allowed me to gain new experience and learn new skills that I wouldn't have had access to at work. It was my way of creating opportunity for myself, which led to finding fulfillment outside of my nine-to-five.

- **Has long-term viability.** I am not going to sugarcoat it—a skill-based side hustle is your best chance at ditching the corporate life and turning it into a full-time gig. This is because when you start this type of side hustle, you have to build your own business. There is no third-party involved that controls how much time or money you can earn, and you have full control over the direction you want to take it.

- **Has higher income potential.** Skill-based side hustles have no income cap. You can build a scalable business especially if you offer a service, you can sell some type of digital product, or you can hire help that can run the business for you without you needing to trade all of your time for money.

Cons of a skill-based side hustle:

- **Requires a lot of effort up front.** Getting any business off the ground is *a lot* of work. There is so much that goes into it, from determining your offerings, strategizing your marketing plan, registering the business—and then actually executing and getting clients or paying customers. It takes time, and that means that there may be a few months at the beginning where you are working on it a lot and not seeing any income.

  I didn't make any money with Break Your Budget for over a year: I had a few paying clients, but any money I made covered the up-front costs I put into it. I started in 2019, and I didn't make *real* profit until 2021. It takes time, so if you are looking to make a quick buck, the skill-based route may not be the one for you.

- **It can become hard to maintain.** When you are working a full-time job, it can be really hard to work eight hours a day and then spend another two to three hours in the evening building a business. Getting any business off the ground requires both mental and physical energy, which is hard to come by after it's entirely drained by your nine-to-five. This balance is challenging and requires intentional, dedicated time in your schedule to focus on building the business.

- **It is emotionally draining.** If I have learned anything on my own journey, it's that entrepreneurship is not for the faint of heart. There are so many ups and downs, especially at the beginning. You see some success, then crickets. Maybe you are building on social and after weeks of consistent effort, it still feels like you are talking to no one. Putting in so much effort with little to no ROI is exhausting—I've been there. The people who power through this and don't give up are the ones you see flaunting their success stories. Be one of those people.

Low/No Skill Side Hustles

If starting a skill-based side hustle feels overwhelming, you have other options. Not only can the thought of starting a business feel crippling, but it may not be something you want to do. That doesn't exclude you from the opportunity to make additional income.

With a low/no skill side hustle, you can make some extra cash on your own time, whenever you want. It doesn't require months of effort, and you can see a return on your time invested fairly quickly. With this type of side-hustle, you are leveraging some type of third party to pick up extra work: it could be driving for rideshare, pet-sitting, shopping for others, delivery, or providing a simple service using a platform like TaskRabbit.

Pros of a low/no skill side hustle:

- **Low barrier to entry.** Anyone with a smartphone or access to the Internet can leverage the tools and apps available to start this type of side hustle. This doesn't necessarily mean it's *easy* and that there are *zero* new skills required—for example, if you drive for Uber you'll need to learn how to use the app and likely need some customer service skills, but it doesn't take as much effort as starting a business on your own.
- **Devote as much time as you want.** Since the infrastructure to make money already exists, you can pick up as many hours as you want. If one week you have a lot of free time, you can leverage that time to work more and ultimately make more money. If your schedule gets busy, you can take a week off with no repercussions. The flexibility and convenience of working whenever you want makes it a lot more appealing than a part-time job; but remember that the onus to make money falls on your discipline to work!
- **Make money right away.** Similar to a part-time job, once you start working you can make money almost immediately. There

is no "waiting period" like a skill-based side hustle where you are planting seeds and creating service packages or products to sell. This is great if you are in a bind and need to make some extra money fast.

Cons of a low/no skill side hustle:

- **Income potential is low.** Since this type of side-hustle is usually based on hourly work and administered through a third party, you don't have as much control over how much money you make, even if you work a lot of hours. If the goal is to replace your full-time income, a low/no skill side hustle isn't a sustainable route.
- **Requires a third-party.** The reason this side hustle is so straightforward is because the business already exists. It's comparable to a part-time job, where you are "hired" by a company to work for them, but the difference is the company you are "hired by" is actually an application that almost everyone can leverage after passing a background check. A few examples include Uber, Lyft, Instacart, Rover, Wag, DoorDash, and TaskRabbit. These companies serve as an intermediary between the service provider (or, side-hustler in this case) and the consumer. The downside of this is that they take a cut of each service provided, limiting your income potential.
- **Not scalable.** As with any type of labor where you are trading your time for money, your income is capped at how many hours you work. With this type of side hustle, you are the sole earner; therefore, the maximum you can earn is limited to the maximum hours you can work per day. There are always ways to improve and become more efficient, but in this case, the limit *does* exist.

How Do You Choose?

After reading through the pros and cons of each avenue, you may already have an idea of which path you'd like to take. But if you're still not sure, here are a few thought starters to help guide the decision.

- *What is your goal of starting a side hustle?* It could be to quit your job, lean into your passions, or just pick up some extra cash. Be honest with yourself and remember, your goals can change after you get started and learn more about what you like to do.
- *How much time do you have?* Time commitment is a major factor. Skill-based side hustles require more up-front time, so be sure that your desire to make additional income isn't urgent if you choose this route. Maybe you only have a few hours per week to dedicate to it, in which case you may want to go the low/no-skill route.
- *How do you want to design your life?* Entrepreneurship isn't for everyone, and a skill-based side hustle is *hard*. Think about what you want your life to look like: maybe you are content at your nine-to-five and want to channel your free time or creativity into an additional endeavor. Or maybe you loathe working for "the man" and are ready to devote the time and energy into starting a business you hope to work on full-time.

I remember when starting Break Your Budget, I had a goal of increasing my income, but it wasn't at the forefront of the decision. I figured, I'll start sharing tips about a topic I already know a lot about, and see where it goes from there. Your side hustle decision isn't life or death, and the direction you choose to move in can—and will—change as you learn and experience more.

Don't put too much pressure on it, and go with what feels right for you in your current phase of life!

Starting a Skill-Based Side Hustle: The One-Person Business

Okay, for those of you reading who have decided to take the skill-based route, you've officially arrived at the fun part: how to get started.

I am going to preface this entire section with a big fat disclaimer: I am no business expert. I didn't go to Harvard, and these tips stem from my own personal experience. That being said, I do think that my experience holds some weight, given that I run a seven-figure side-hustle-turned-full-time-job that I've built and scaled entirely on my own!

As you read in the introduction of this chapter, Break Your Budget (BYB) started on social media and has been monetized via a few different avenues: selling digital products, working with brands, and now writing books and leveraging the opportunities that come along with that.

My experience building a business is within the online, *solopreneurship* niche. This means that I have created a one-person digital business, and I am the sole operator and engine behind everything you see related to BYB. I don't have a storefront, my overhead costs are low, and no one works for me: I run the show behind my computer.

This is the type of side hustle I am going to explain how to start. No storefront, employees, or 15-page business plan required.

Let's dive in.

The Process

Ultimately, starting a super-profitable one-person business isn't really complicated. It can be boiled down into a simple four-step process that outlines the idea, the product or service, the implementation, and the ability to scale. As I explain each layer of this process, I am going to use Break Your Budget as a case study to provide a real-world example you can use as inspiration and leverage for your own one-person business idea.

Keep in mind, this business model can be applied to *anything*. Any interest, hobby, or industry can be monetized, from gardening to gaming to knitting and everything in between. No interest is off-limits and the opportunities are endless. When ideating, it's important to note that most profitable and successful businesses fall within one of the three major pillars of a good life: health, wealth, and relationships.

Phase 1: The Idea (aka the Problem or the Goal)

Every business solves some type of problem: if the problem didn't exist, there would be no need for a product or service to be sold as the solution. To get started, first think about your personal interests, hobbies, and experiences. What problems have you faced? Are there common questions or issues that you and your peers encounter? This doesn't have to be siloed to your personal life: think professionally, socially, and anywhere in between.

If you're stuck, reverse-engineer the question: rather than think about a problem, think about the goals others (or yourself) want to achieve—in all areas of life—and how you can help someone get there.

Another perspective to take is to identify a topic area you already know really well and find a problem within it. Using BYB as the example, a topic I already knew very well was personal finance, and I could talk to a variety of different subtopics such as budgeting and investing within the broader topic area.

Beyond that, I identified both a goal and a problem within the general topic I already had knowledge of. A goal many young adults have is to achieve their definition of financial freedom. The problem they face is a lack of knowledge and/or tools available to save and invest their money to reach financial freedom.

How do I help them solve that problem and reach their goal? By teaching them how to budget through educational content that is delivered via a variety of platforms such as social media, a podcast, email newsletter, and a book, as well as providing the tools (for a fee, of course) for them to implement those lessons and apply them to their lives.

The goal of this exercise is to identify the problem you will solve, along with the niche, subniche, and target audience you will be focusing on.

Your niche and subniche are those topic areas you already know really well. For me, that was personal finance (niche) and budgeting (subniche). Because the problem I solve is one I faced in my own life, my target audience was myself and my peers. To hone this down, I identified the target audience as young professionals.

When working through this process, ensure that the problem or goal you identify is significant enough to justify creating a product or service to solve it. It also needs to have a large enough target audience that would be willing to pay for a solution. You don't need to reinvent the wheel; you could instead innovate on an already existing solution that could be improved or changed based on your own experience, expertise, or perspective.

Break Your Budget Case Study

At this point you know that Break Your Budget was born out of a problem I identified in my own life and from my friends and coworkers around me: young professionals have no idea what to do with their finances when they start working.

Even though I studied finance in college and worked in the industry, I was still struggling to properly budget my paycheck and work toward my financial goals. I knew it was important, but I didn't know *what to do*—so I looked to others for validation and help. The issue? No one else knew what to do either, and money is so taboo that there was no real information online to access.

And thus, Break Your Budget came to be. It was my way of learning as I went—taking the relevant information I learned at work and applying it to my life, while simultaneously sharing what I was doing online to help other people. Sharing helped me identify the subniche areas of interest that I was both interested in and good at. I discovered how passionate I am about budgeting, from optimization to automation and everything in between, and as a result I focused my attention on solving this problem specifically.

At its earliest stages, there were no products or services. I primarily shared my educational content on social media with the intent of building a following of young professionals who also struggled with budgeting and needed guidance. I knew the direction I was heading in involved a product or service, because there were so many people who were interested in hearing what I had to say and learning more about money. The validation of my idea, and ultimately the product and service I offered, came from building the audience on social media and answering questions from them every day.

As I continued to share more, I spent more time talking with my followers and understanding their problems. With that information, I could ideate on solutions to those problems that would help them reach their goals. This is where my templates—such as the Personal Finance Dashboard and the Own Your Career Template—began.

The lesson from my personal journey is that if you have a general idea of what you may want to start with, *just start* and ideate from there. I knew that there was a need for personal finance education, but initially I wasn't sure how I was going to introduce a solution. By taking action and focusing on educating first, I discovered solvable problems and created offers that filled the gap. You don't need to have a perfect idea and a perfect solution from the beginning, and I'd actually advise against it because it's likely it will change anyway.

Phase 2: The Product or Service (aka the Solution)

Every product or service is a *solution* to a problem. Let's use the most basic example: a chair. A chair exists so there is a place to sit. It solves the problem of not wanting to stand or sit on the ground. Now, let's think about a couch. Is a couch an entirely *new* product, or is it an innovation of an existing solution to a problem that helps people in a different way?

Once you've identified your niche, your problem, and the goal you are helping your target audience achieve, it's time to think about the solution, which is the product or service you create. It needs to add value to the consumer; this can be done through education and teaching, problem-solving, saving time, or improving efficiency. Think about how you can make someone else's life easier: this is how you get people to pay.

There are endless options for products and services you can offer. Generally, starting with offering a service, whether it be a consultation or a done-for-you service, is a great place to start because you can work with clients and gain an even deeper understanding of the problems they face and what is standing in their way of success.

As you work with more and more people, you will be able to identify themes and then create products that can help solve those problems without you needing to be directly involved. You don't need to reinvent the wheel; if an offer that you like or resonate with already exists, think about ways you can enhance it or add your own personal perspective or twist to make it different. Going back to the chair example—is a couch *really* a new product, or is it an innovation of an existing product? The answer is the latter.

Break Your Budget Case Study

In its early stages, I offered one-on-one budgeting consultations as a service. From the solution lens, this service existed to educate and help other young professionals build their first budget and learn sustainable habits to implement into their lives to actually stick to that budget. To implement these sessions, I priced out an hour of my time, had each client fill out a survey in advance, and then I would put together a game plan for the call. After the call, I'd write down all of the action steps discussed and then send over a more detailed version of the call plan for them to follow and implement on their own time.

Through these consultations, I discovered that one of the biggest missing links was a tool to properly aggregate their finances and create their first budget. At the time, I just directed them to a free budgeting template or app online. Eventually I noticed that more and more people were asking for a tool at the end of my consultations, and the idea that has now become the bread and butter of my business was born: create a budget template for sale.

That is how the Personal Finance Dashboard (PFD), my now signature template, was first created. I built the template with my own needs at the forefront: what was missing from the other budgeting tools I've used? How can I aggregate different elements of my financial life in a way that enables me to make better financial decisions? And beyond that, what questions were being asked most frequently in my consultations and how can this template help alleviate or solve them?

I used the answers to these questions to guide the creation of this template, which has now grossed hundreds of thousands of dollars in revenue. Plus, it served as a jumping off point for other digital templates and online courses that solve *other* problems that I've gathered through continuous feedback and questions from users.

Starting out with consultations where I was selling a service enabled me to create a product that had a validated need *and* that people were ready to buy. Plus, going back to my earlier point, I wasn't reinventing the wheel. Is the Personal Finance Dashboard the first and only budgeting template to ever exist? Of course not! But it is my own twist that is designed and suited to my brand and that differentiates it from the others on the market.

Phase 3: The Implementation (aka the Marketing)

Marketing your product or service is your opportunity to make people care about what you are offering. There are three main pillars of marketing an offer: brand, place, and promotion.

- Branding is *how* your business and service is perceived. It's the outward image you project via your various streams of advertising. You can make this personal, professional, or somewhere in between. Remember, people buy from people, so adding a personal flair can make a huge difference.
- Place is *where* you do your advertising. In the past, businesses would need to purchase ad space in magazines or on TV in order to get their product in front of consumers. Now, we have a wonderful tool called *the Internet*, which is free to use and can be leveraged to advertise at no cost. I'll talk about this in a minute.
- Promotion is *how* you advertise your offer. This is where you want to highlight the problem the target consumer is facing and position your offer as the solution. The goal is to evoke emotion, because emotional connection increases your chances of making a sale.

Place and promotion have a lot of overlap, especially when building an online business. The best place to advertise and promote your business? Social media. Let's talk about it.

Content Marketing

Social media marketing and influencer marketing are still relatively new to the advertising ecosystem. However, there is a new subset of social media marketing that is still in its infancy stage: content marketing.

Content marketing is different from influencer marketing because the goal isn't to leverage a personal brand to advertise *another business's* product or service; it's to create *your own* brand

and use it to advertise *your own* business. Let's break down exactly what content marketing is.

First and foremost, content marketing is a vehicle for advertising your offer by creating content on social media. The type of content and the platform utilized is up to you. There are so many different social media platforms that exist today from Instagram to TikTok to Facebook, and I'm sure by the time you are reading this book there will be another platform we have all culturally adopted.

More importantly, it's a way for you to create your brand, tell your story, and showcase your expertise and the value you can bring to consumers in an organic way. There are so many different types of content that can be leveraged, whether it be educational, inspirational, or entertaining. By creating content and sharing it on social media, you have the opportunity to share your unique perspective and approach to whatever problem you are solving, while simultaneously building a connection with consumers and ideally, growing an audience of ready-to-buy followers.

Now I know what you're thinking: *But what if I don't want to be an influencer or post on the Internet?*

Content marketing is a subniche of influencing, but it isn't a path to becoming an *influencer*, and it's distinctly different. As I noted earlier, an influencer is a vehicle for advertising someone else's business behind the facade of a seemingly relatable yet aspirational person. Generally speaking, the majority of influencers don't have their own product or service that they are selling; they make money from working with brands and advertising the brand's products on their page.

A *content creator*—someone who utilizes content marketing—is a person who is leveraging social media to tell a story and build a business. It's a tool to advertise *your own offer* rather than someone else's. As a result, you don't have to share what you're wearing or what products you're using or the intimate details of your life. You can simply post content teaching people about your interests, telling them how you overcame the challenges you can help them with, and presenting the solution.

When it comes to marketing, it's important to remember that if you aren't seen, you won't make any sales. You have to get comfortable with having an online presence in some way, or else how will anyone know that you have a product or service to offer?

The beauty of content marketing is that it can be entirely free if you're willing to put yourself out there. This is a far cry from what marketing used to look like, where you had to create a polished ad, buy a placement for it, and then cross your fingers and hope that the right people not only see it but are convinced to purchase as a result. With content marketing, you can create a piece of content—whether it be a static post for Instagram or a video for TikTok—and the odds that the content ends up in front of a group of like-minded people is a lot higher.

Over time, and with consistent posting, you can build an audience of engaged followers who are interested in what you are talking about and who can become potential customers. It's more targeted than traditional marketing, and in many cases totally free.

Content Marketing Strategy to Get Started

If you're feeling overwhelmed or have no idea where to start with content marketing, no worries. I am going to break down a simple strategy you can implement to get the ball rolling. Once you start, you can iterate and change your strategy as you learn.

There are three main pillars to a strong content marketing strategy:

- **Your story:** this is who you are
- **Your lessons:** this is what you are teaching
- **Your offer:** this is what you are selling

The goal is to incorporate all three of these pillars into the marketing content that you post. It enables your audience of potential followers and customers to get to know you, learn from you as you build authority, and better understand how you can help them.

Your Story

Remember when I said people buy from people? Your audience needs to know who you are and why you are talking about your topic. Your goal from telling your story is to become relatable and showcase how you used to struggle with your problem, and ultimately solved it using whatever solution you are offering. A simple formula to tell your story is to show the obstacle you faced in a relatable way, highlight the turning point, and then show the steps you took to solve the problem.

Story = obstacle + turning point + steps to address. This can be even more effective if you make the steps to address the problem formulaic, because people love a three-step solution, a framework, or a process that is easy to follow.

Your Lessons

An excellent way to build authority and become a recognized expert is to teach and educate without selling. Obviously the ultimate goal is for someone to purchase a product or service from your business, but in order to build trust and show them that your product or service is worth the money, they need to get value from you for free. Aside from sharing your story, your main focus with content marketing should be to provide value with the expectation of nothing in return. This means using your content to share implementable tips that people can use to get quick wins and validate that you know what you're talking about.

Your Offer

Part of your content marketing strategy is to showcase and talk about your offer so your audience knows that it exists. That being said, people don't like to be advertised to, so there is a method to the madness to effectively market your offer without coming across overly salesy, and it boils down to direct and indirect selling via what is called a call-to-action (CTA). An example of a CTA is "Go click the link in my bio to purchase X" or "Book a call with me via my calendar link."

Direct selling is a hard sell: It means you directly state a CTA and tell your audience about your offer. Incorporating direct selling content is important because it is your opportunity to explicitly highlight your offer and drive people directly to it. That being said, these tend to be the least popular pieces of content because, as I mentioned, people don't like to be sold to and are less likely to passively engage.

Indirect selling is a softer sell: it could be showcasing your product in the background of a video, or throwing in a quick CTA at the end of an educational piece of content. This content has a much higher chance of performing well, getting attention, or even going viral, so incorporating indirect selling is a great way to get your offer in front of more people. I use indirect selling *all the time* with the Personal Finance Dashboard by showing it on my computer screen in videos, but not directly calling attention to it.

To bring all three of these pillars together into an effective content marketing strategy, a great starting goal is to share one piece of content within each pillar every week. Once you nail that cadence, you can continue to increase your content output until you find the optimal amount of posting that works for you and helps you generate sales.

This content can be video, audio, photo, or written content—it depends on what social media platforms you enjoy, where your target audience generally consumes content, and your comfort level with the various media. If you don't want to do video content, you can create LinkedIn posts or Instagram carousels. If you love video and audio, you can make TikToks or a podcast. Choose one or two media to start with and grow from there.

Break Your Budget Case Study

I was never a social media person. I never liked having my photo taken, I hate being the center of attention, and design and aesthetic are not my strong suits. Yet somehow, I've ended up with a very large social media following—some may call me a financial influencer, but I prefer to call myself a content creator.

Social media has entirely changed my life. It is the main vehicle for advertising my products, but it's also created opportunities for me that I never could have imagined (I mean, I am now an author). All that to say, if you're hesitant to leverage content marketing to start your side hustle that you hope to turn into your full-time job, don't be.

When I first started my side hustle, I posted pictures of myself on Instagram with long captions explaining various personal finance topics or sharing how I was using my money. I took time to record Instagram stories going deeper on these topics, because at the time, video content didn't reign supreme. This was within my comfort zone and was manageable for me to stick with consistently while balancing my full-time job.

Over time, my online presence morphed alongside the ever changing landscape of social media. I jumped on the TikTok bandwagon and started sharing educational video content, which helped me amass a large following in a relatively short period of time. I continued to share content on Instagram but evolved from sharing pictures of myself to sharing static graphics and reels.

All of the content I shared did one of the following: educated my audience, highlighted my personal experience, or inspired my audience to take action. This strategy, combined with subtle product placement and the occasional "Go get

(continued)

the PFD linked in my bio!" enabled me to sell thousands of budgeting templates and replace my nine-to-five income. If you need examples, there are thousands of posts across my various social media channels that you can use as inspiration on your own journey.

No matter which way you slice it, content marketing works. It isn't an overnight solution, but with consistent effort and strategy, it will help you build a strong brand identity, showcase your skills, and highlight how your solution can help solve whatever problem your ideal consumer faces.

Phase 4: Scalability: (aka Ecosystem for Growth)

The last layer of this process is your ability to scale, which is how you grow your business and sell more without doing significantly more work. This could be an entire chapter or even book in and of itself, but I am going to highlight the three key aspects you need to nail to scale your business:

- **Content system:** how to systemize and reuse content to cross-post on different platforms
- **Email funnel:** leveraging email to sell on autopilot
- **Digital products:** packaging up your service to sell as a product

Content System

Now that you understand the value of content marketing and have a baseline strategy for getting started, it's important to learn how to leverage the content you are already creating to grow on various platforms.

While I recommend choosing one or two platforms to start out on, as your business grows, you will likely want (or need) to get in front of more eyes. A great way to do this is to build a presence on different social media platforms, because different people use different media, and not everyone consumes content on each one.

To do this, you don't need to come up with a ton of different content ideas or pieces of content. You can simply cross-post content you've already created, or shapeshift the content to fit each medium accordingly.

For example, with BYB, I created a piece of content on TikTok about the task-management system I explained in Chapter 6. This video performed very well, so I decided to save the video and post it on Instagram reels, where it also performed very well. From there, I took the script that I followed and turned the video into both a carousel post for Instagram, and a written post for LinkedIn. I also elaborated on the script and turned it into an email newsletter and a podcast episode. See what I am getting at? That one idea generated more than five pieces of content for me across a variety of different media.

To scale your content strategy and get in front of more people, you don't need to create *more*—you need to create *differently*. Look at each piece of content you create as an idea that can be transformed into a variety of pieces of content that can be cross-posted on different platforms to reach more people with less work.

Email Funnels

Email marketing can be super complex, but it is an incredibly effective tool for sales conversion. Building an email list is a fantastic way to grow your audience from social media and sell to them while you sleep.

Here's the quick and dirty description for how to do this:

Step 1: Create a valuable freebie. A freebie is a piece of free content that you make available in exchange for an email address. It can be access to a video, a PDF guide, a template—get creative. The goal of the freebie is to provide value related to your offer in exchange for someone's email. With BYB, I have a variety of free guides related to topics I get asked about often, such as investing and high-yield savings accounts.

Step 2: Build a basic email automation. An email automation is a sequence of emails that provides value to the user. Within this automation, you can share value, talk about your offer, provide an exclusive discount or bonus, and hopefully make some sales. There are tons of free selling sequences available online, so do some googling, and try to find one that suits your style and offer. Make sure you change it up a bit and make it sound like you so it doesn't come across as inauthentic.

Step 3: Send people to your free guide often. The goal with an email funnel is to get as many people to opt-in by downloading your freebie as possible. That way, they will be automatically taken through your automated email sequence to learn about your offer and have the opportunity to purchase it, without you needing to do anything more than create the sequence and market the freebie.

This is an incredibly oversimplified explanation of email marketing and email funnels, but you get the gist. Email is an excellent way to automate your marketing strategy and sell your offer without any additional lift beyond generating opt-ins!

Digital Products

At this point in the book I've touched on digital products a bit, but the key message I want to get across is that a digital product is an amazing way to earn mostly passive income. I say *mostly* because true passive income doesn't really exist: you still need to create content and market your digital product.

But the beauty of a digital product is that once you create it—which does require a lot of work up front—you can sell it over and over and over again to as many people as possible without exchanging your time for money. There is no limit to how many you can sell and, ultimately, how much money you can make. Unlike a service where someone is purchasing a defined period of your time, a digital product is purchased and the value comes from the consumer implementing it on their own time. It could be a digital template, an online course, or an e-book; the options are endless.

If you have a successful service and have either reached a ceiling on how much money you can make or would just like more time in your day, you can package that service into a digital product and sell it. That is why there is so much value in starting with a service first, because you can create a process, deeply understand your target audience's problems, and create the framework for the solution in a way that generates results. Then, you can turn it into a digital product and replace that service with the product itself.

Using BYB as an example, I have created an entire suite of digital products from templates to online courses. Each of these products was born from my original service: budgeting consultations. Those consultations taught me so much about my ideal consumer and the problems they face that I was able to create my own process for solving them.

Now I sell my digital products through my cross-platform content marketing strategy as well as with my email funnels and generate hundreds of thousands of dollars in sales each year.

By the time you've reached the point of scaling your business with digital products, you are basically a one-person business expert! Building a business is hard work, and it's not for everyone. But for those of you who are serious about entrepreneurship and creating your own path, it is so worth it!

Key Takeaways

- There are two distinct types of side hustles: a skill-based side hustle, and a low/no skill side hustle. Skill-based side hustles leverage a specific skill set or expertise to start a business, whereas a low/no skill side hustle leverages a third party to make money.
- When choosing a side hustle to pursue, get clear on your goal of starting, how much time you realistically have to commit to it, and how you want to design your lifestyle. If you want to build a business to leave corporate, you may want to commit to a skill-based side hustle. If you want to pick up some extra cash, a low/no skill side hustle may be a better option.
- There are four phases to starting a digital one-person business: the idea, the product or service, the implementation, and the

ability to scale. This process can be applied to any niche or industry, but many successful businesses apply to health, wealth, and relationships.

- When ideating on a business idea and product or service to offer, you don't need to reinvent the wheel. How can you enhance or iterate on an existing product/service by adding your own perspective or twist to make it unique and different?
- There are three pillars of marketing your offer: brand, place, and promotion. A great place to accomplish all three pillars is by implementing content marketing across various social media apps.
- The goal of content marketing is to create your own brand and use it to advertise your own business by creating educational and personal content to share on social media channels. Focus on creating content that tells your story, shares your lessons, and advertises your offer.
- Scaling your business requires systems, including a content marketing system to repurpose your content across platforms and an email funnel, along with a digital product that you can sell without trading your valuable time for money.

Chapter 8

Taking Your Side Hustle to the Next Level

Leaving my corporate job to pursue entrepreneurship and focus on Break Your Budget full-time was the best decision I have ever made in my life, and I don't say that lightly. You already know that I struggled in corporate and my real passion was, and still is, my business.

Entrepreneurship has completely changed my perspective on work, life, and the synergies that exist between those two pillars of being. Truthfully, I am an entirely different person after two years of self-employment, and the corporate version of Michela that used to be a major part of my identity doesn't exist anymore.

I used to view my job as a core pillar of who I was. I equated so much of my worth with how other people perceived what I was doing. I wanted to sound important because it made me *feel* important. Unfortunately, it also made me feel incredibly unhappy, depressed, and hopeless about my future and how I'd ever truly feel both satisfied with my work and financially comfortable.

All that being said, building a business that is strong enough to support you on its own is a challenge, and my journey has not been a walk in the park. Here is an overview of the true timeline and sequence of events that took Break Your Budget from an idea to a full-fledged business.

The Evolution of Break Your Budget

July 2019: Created my first business Instagram handle, @Break YourBudget. I began posting daily and sharing tips about budgeting and investing. I knew nothing about social media and thought that if I posted a lot, more people would see it. I was working a corporate job in investment consulting (what I originally thought was my "dream job") and hated it.

November 2019: Landed my first one-on-one budgeting client. She signed on for a three-month retainer, where we would meet weekly for an hour, and I helped her unpack her money struggles, build a budget, stay accountable, and implement sustainable financial routines.

January 2020: Landed two more one-on-one budgeting clients for my three-month retainer program and began accepting individualized one-on-one budgeting consults. At this time I was still posting on Instagram regularly and began incorporating some more strategy into the posts to attract clients.

March 2020: The pandemic hit, and I moved to my parents' house. I had also recently landed a new job paying me $30k more than my prior job, so the pressure to make money with my budgeting consults dwindled. I was struggling with growth on social media and feeling really defeated, but I kept posting anyway because I had so much more time as a result of the pandemic.

July 2020: I created the first iteration of the Personal Finance Dashboard. After months of working with budgeting clients and not having a tool to provide, along with my own desire to create a budgeting spreadsheet for myself, I started working on the PFD. After about three weeks of building, testing, and creating a sales page, I put it up for sale for 50 percent off. I sold five of them and was psyched.

December 2020: I posted my first TikTok. It was a video of me making fun of the "crypto bro" persona and letting people know to follow me for *real* finance tips that would actually help them. It got 60k views, and I started growing followers right away.

January 2021: I hit 100k followers on TikTok after posting videos explaining various budgeting and financial concepts. I was utilizing a very specific style of video where I filmed myself writing on my notepad but didn't show my face. It made it a lot easier for me to push out content without feeling embarrassed, because I was scared that people from my personal life or my job would see it.

February 2021: I landed my first paid brand deal with a budgeting app. They asked me what my rate was for one video, and I had no idea, so I just said $1,000. They agreed to pay me $900 and I could. Not. Believe it. It was at this point that I started to realize I could be working on something that might be serious.

March 2021: My videos on TikTok continued to perform well, so I began setting up systems in my business to start selling the Personal Finance Dashboard and booking more one-on-one clients. I took an email marketing class, created an email funnel and a freebie, and started plugging the freebie at the end of my TikTok videos. I gained 2,000 subscribers in about a week and started seeing more sales on my template.

August 2021: I moved to LA and continued to work my corporate job while focusing on Break Your Budget in my free time. I was working East Coast hours on the West Coast, so at 2 p.m. I would switch my attention from my full-time job to Break Your Budget. I also landed my first multi-month brand deal and was feeling super confident. At this point, I was making around $5k per month from brand deals, and an additional $5k–$6k from the PFD. I also finally reached 10,000 followers on Instagram (after two years!).

November 2021: I hit my first $10k month in template sales. This was a result of a very strategic and focused social media plan combined with a Black Friday sale. It turned out to be a major turning point in my business.

February 2022: I began connecting with other creators I met online and learned about various opportunities and brands they were working with. I also attended a Super Bowl party sponsored by one of the brands I worked with, and it completely changed my perspective on available opportunities in the online space. I was passed over for a promotion at work that I felt like I deserved and was told that I would not be promoted until the end of the year.

March 2022: I made the decision to leave my corporate job. At this point, I had consistent brand partnerships coming through my pipeline, and I had been consistently hitting $10k minimum months on my template sales. I also had recently signed my first book deal and was feeling confident—yet terrified—with this decision.

April 2022: I formally left my corporate job and began full-time self-employment. It felt as if I had so much to do and nothing to do at the same time. I didn't realize how difficult it would be to structure my days, get organized, and find a workflow that worked for me.

And now, fast-forward a few years later, I've scaled Break Your Budget to become a seven-figure business. I've published my first book and am writing my second book. I've created a variety of digital products that have amassed hundreds of thousands of dollars in sales, and I've worked with tons of brands I never could have dreamed of.

It took me nearly three years to reach a point where I could comfortably leave my nine-to-five job. While my journey may be longer than others, it exemplifies how difficult it can be to truly build a business that you can rely on with recurring and diversified revenue streams.

Leaving a stable, full-time job stacked with benefits for self-employment is terrifying. In this chapter, I dive deep on how to prepare for taking this leap with confidence, as well as how to manage your business finances. You'll walk away equipped with the tools you need to take control of your decision to pursue entrepreneurship full-time and never look back.

Self-Employment versus Corporate Work: Let's Talk About It

The Internet glorifies self-employment. You've likely seen the "laptop lifestyle" at some point on social media: this includes some variation of working-from-Bali or another tropical beach, generating passive income, and spending your time jumping off cliffs, drinking smoothies, and living in uninterrupted bliss for the rest of eternity.

This is not the reality of self-employment. In fact, self-employment in many ways can look very similar to working a nine-to-five with the main difference being the person who tells you what to do isn't your manager, it's *you*.

I absolutely love working for myself, and I've never felt more like myself than over the last two years of being my own boss. But, as with anything, self-employment comes with its own set of challenges, and if you think leaving your corporate job to work for yourself will solve your career problems, it probably won't. So before I get into the details, I want to talk about some of the pros and cons of self-employment so that you don't make the leap blind.

The Drawbacks of Self-Employment

Let's start with the cons:

- **Unpredictability.** Arguably, to me, the hardest part of self-employment is the unpredictability. In a corporate job, you have a relatively set schedule, you can expect a direct deposit every two weeks and know exactly how much it will be, and you get predictable benefits such as a 401(k) and health insurance.

   When pursuing any form of entrepreneurship, you give all of that up. From a financial standpoint, your pay frequency and amount you earn can vary dramatically month to month. There are ways to mitigate these swings, but there could be instances where you make an entire month's worth of income in a day, or a month where you earn $0.

   Beyond the financial unpredictability, work un predictability is also prevalent. Learning your busy and slow seasons and spacing out work accordingly can take years to solidify. If there is a fire drill on something you are working on, addressing it can come at the sacrifice of missing a deadline or passing up on another paid opportunity. The lack of predictability requires a combination of serious planning, organization, and mental strength that not everyone can handle.

- **"Always on" mentality.** This is especially prevalent with social media–based businesses, because culturally we all exist online. But beyond that, when you run a business there is usually *always* something more that you could be doing. This makes it hard to draw the line between work and your personal life and can also make it challenging to take fully unplugged vacation time. I haven't taken a completely unplugged vacation in over three years. This is largely because there is an expectation that I am present on social media, but also because sharing my life and posting consistently is how I make money. It's not something I am proud of, but it's extremely common in entrepreneurship.

- **Owning everything.** When starting any type of business, you have two options: do everything yourself or pay someone else to do it for you. Hiring help is a major commitment, and to this day, I haven't hired anyone besides a contractor who briefly helped me edit videos for YouTube. This means that I am the CEO, CFO, CMO, CSO, project manager, copywriter, video and podcast editor, lead creative, and accountant for Break Your Budget. I do *everything*—and for the things I didn't already know how to do, I had to learn. Putting money on the line to hire someone is a lot of pressure, and finding good help is really hard.

The Benefits of Self-Employment

These cons are all solvable problems, albeit they can be challenging to address. That being said, there are countless pros to self-employment, and I personally feel like they outweigh all of the cons.

- **Control over your life.** I cannot emphasize enough how amazing it is to have control over your life. To not be bound to a set schedule or have to answer to a manager breathing down your neck is one of the most freeing experiences, and I wish for everyone who struggles at work to be able to experience it.

The beauty of self-employment is that you get to decide what you work on, who you work with, and what you do every single day. If you want to take a half day, you can. If you need to take a day off to do errands or get your life in order, you can. If you're tired and want to sleep in, you can. It's a wonderful feeling, and it has completely changed my entire personality. I am so much happier, flexible, and agreeable knowing that I get to decide how I live my life.

- **Earning potential.** With a corporate job, your income is capped at your salary. When you work for yourself, your earning potential is infinite. If you look at the wealthiest and most successful people in the world, they are either C-suite executives of major Fortune 500 companies (which, let's be real, that is like 0.1% of the workforce), or they are entrepreneurs with their own businesses and companies.

  This is especially true with online, one-person businesses because there are billions of people with access to the Internet and your overhead costs are very low. This means you have an enormous market to capitalize on, an essentially endless list of opportunity and ideas, and the ability to make very high profit margins.

- **Creativity.** Most corporate roles are very specific and siloed within a certain area of expertise. A major benefit of self-employment is the ability to lean into different interests and passions, and then leverage your own creativity to monetize.

  Using myself as the example, when I worked my finance job, I was obviously interested in finance. But I was also interested in marketing, productivity, and social media, and those were areas that I would have never had the opportunity to explore had I continued down on that path. I love to write, I love to create, I love to plan, I love to build routines and now that I work for myself, I get to spend time doing those things *and* share it with people.

  Exercising your creative brain has so many benefits, and it can lead to higher job satisfaction over time through experiencing new challenges, the ability to problem-solve, and learn new things in areas you actually care about.

I could go on and on about how amazing self-employment is all day, or I could tell you how to start financially preparing to make the leap. Let's dive in.

Financially Preparing to Leave Your Job

One of the biggest mistakes any entrepreneur can make is to leave a full-time job too soon. Conventional advice tells you to "go all in" and "take big risks" when you are pursuing a dream.

This is a bad idea, because it puts an enormous amount of unnecessary pressure on you to generate enough income to make ends meet, which can hinder creativity, lead to bad decision-making, and ultimately cripple your success.

If your true goal is to eventually leave your corporate job and pursue your business full-time, then you need to be strategic about taking the leap. It requires careful consideration and planning and should not be done with haste. Giving up a stable paycheck and taking a chance on yourself is a huge decision that can't be taken lightly.

There are four considerations to plan for *before* you give your boss your two-week notice. I know you may be eager to escape a toxic job or simply pour yourself into your passions, but you shouldn't do so with your livelihood on the line. Ensuring that each of these four bases are covered will make the transition a lot smoother!

Consideration #1: Revenue Streams

When it comes to your revenue streams, there are two pillars to think about: diversifying your revenue and creating recurring revenue.

Diversifying your revenue means creating multiple revenue streams within your business. Think about the theme of diversification in this context as reducing risk; if you are reliant on only making money through brand deals, and then your Instagram gets hacked, all of a sudden you have no way of making money. You can't put all your eggs in one basket, and so your goal from the start should be to create and solidify two to three income streams that you can rely on.

Beyond diversifying your revenue, you need to create recurring revenue. This provides a degree of income stability, so you aren't starting each month from zero and scrambling every day to make your next paycheck. There are many different ways to create recurring income, whether it be signing a multiple-month contract or requiring clients to commit to a three-month retainer.

If you don't have two to three income streams that you can rely on for at least three months in advance, you aren't ready to leave your job.

Consideration #2: Business Safety Net

A *business safety net* is the equivalent of an emergency fund, but for your business. This is dedicated money that has been set aside to cover business expenses and/or your personal expenses if you have major fluctuations in your revenue.

Fluctuations are totally normal and should be expected. But as a result, it's your job to be prepared for them. This means that you should have at least three months of both business and personal expenses set aside in a separate account *before* you even consider leaving your job.

If you don't have substantial funds to protect yourself in case of a business fluctuation or failure, you aren't ready to leave your job.

Consideration #3: Replacing Your Income

This might be a hot take, but I don't believe anyone should even *consider* full-time entrepreneurship until they've replaced their monthly and annual salary in revenue. In fact, it's financially irresponsible to consider any other option.

There is no need to rush something that you are building to last a long time. Take as much time as you need to grow your revenue, diversify your income, and fully replace your monthly and annual pay. Not only will this provide you the financial security you need to navigate the transition and maintenance of your business, but it will also allow you to fully focus on growth when you do finally make that leap without the pressure of making ends meet.

In fact, I'd argue that you should actually be making *more* per month and year from your business before you're truly ready to dive in full-time. This is because revenue isn't really indicative of business health; you need to consider your expenses as well as taxes, which will surprise you if you haven't properly prepared.

I didn't even consider leaving my full-time job until Break Your Budget made six figures in annual revenue, and I was making $10k/month consistently on my template for five months before I put in my notice. I also had secured a six-month brand contract, which essentially bought me the time to figure things out if all of a sudden, my template sales stopped.

If you have not completely replaced your income with your business revenue, you aren't ready to leave your job.

Consideration #4: Replacing Your Benefits

Benefits are usually one of the main reasons people stay in a corporate job longer than they either want to or need to. This is totally understandable, because often the benefits you get from a nine-to-five such as health insurance and a 401(k) can be incredibly valuable.

That being said, many of these benefits are replaceable, and if leaving your job is something you are seriously considering or preparing for, then it's your responsibility to not only explore your options for replacing them but also how much it will cost you.

There are two major benefits you lose when you leave your job: health insurance and a retirement plan.

Health Insurance

Health insurance can be very expensive, depending on your current health, family, and/or dependents. For the first 18 months after you leave your job, you are eligible to take advantage of COBRA, which allows workers and their families to stay enrolled in an employer-sponsored health plan. However, this can be very expensive, and you may be able to find a more affordable option elsewhere.

Many states have a health care marketplace where you can shop online for your plan as well as explore and compare your various options. You can also explore federal plans, but these may be limited depending on your income. Another option is to purchase a plan directly through a private insurer, although these tend to be more expensive and may provide less coverage.

Ultimately, you need to understand your health insurance options *before* you give it up. And when you do reach the point where you're ready to put in your notice, make sure you use up all your health care benefits before they run out! Go get that last appointment, see the specialist, and refill your prescriptions.

Retirement Plans

Beyond health care, think about your retirement plan. Just because you are self-employed doesn't mean retirement goes out the window. Before you leave, refresh yourself on your employer's 401(k) structure, matching program, and vesting schedule; it would be a shame to leave a month before your 401(k) matches fully vest, especially if you don't need to! I share more about 401(k) strategy and vesting schedules in my book *Own Your Money*.

> When I was preparing to put in my two weeks, I realized that my proposed last day would be one week before my 401(k) matches hit the second tier of my vesting schedule. Because of this, I decided to wait an extra week so that I could ensure I'd walk away with that money. Pay attention to these details so you don't walk away leaving any money on the table.

Once you do leave your full-time job, you still need to consider your options for retirement saving. As a self-employed person, you have options from a SEP IRA, a solo 401(k), or a Roth/traditional

IRA. The challenge is determining which option fits your specific situation, and the factors will vary depending on your revenue and business structure. I recommend consulting with a CPA or CFP to select the most optimal retirement option. Do this *before* you leave your job!

Beyond replacing your major benefits such as health insurance and a 401(k), make sure that you use up all the benefits you have access to. Take the extra day of PTO, make sure you collect any bonuses owed to you, and schedule those doctors' appointments.

If you have not carefully considered your plan for replacing your benefits such as health insurance and a 401(k), you aren't ready to leave your job.

Business Finances: Everything You Need to Know

Whether you are well-versed with your personal finances or not, business finances are an entirely new ball game. I always thought that being financially literate in my personal life meant that I would easily be able to grasp bookkeeping and accounting and business-related financial decisions, but I've learned through a lot of trial and error that business finances are entirely different.

When it comes to managing your business finances, there are a lot of things you need to pay attention to, from your bookkeeping to your taxes to your profitability and everything in between. Plus, you're going to need a system to manage it all so when tax season comes around you aren't unknowingly committing any crimes.

I am not a tax expert nor an accountant. This is a quick and dirty business finance rundown, and there are definitely aspects of business finances, registration, and taxes that I am not going to touch on because it is not my area of expertise. The goal is for you to understand the key elements of business finances, learn what to pay attention to from the beginning, and understand the importance of outsourcing your questions to the experts.

Before I get into the details, here is the single most important lesson to walk away with when it comes to business finances: *keep everything related to your business separate from your personal accounts*.

The second you decide to start your business, open a separate bank account and credit card. Keep everything business-related in one place, and never ever intermix your business and personal expenses or accounts! Doing this makes it possible for you to have a clear picture of your business cash flow, financial health, and provides an extra layer of protection in case you ever find yourself in legal trouble. Don't question it; just do it.

Bookkeeping

Bookkeeping is just a glorified version of revenue and expense tracking, with a few extra steps. For probably about a year, I thought that I needed to outsource all of my bookkeeping because I was afraid that I had no idea what to do. What I realized is that bookkeeping is actually quite simple when you are set up correctly.

There are two ways you can go about your bookkeeping: with a spreadsheet or with software. When Break Your Budget was in its infancy stage, I actually created my own bookkeeping template to use as a riff off the Personal Finance Dashboard. It has its own profit and loss statement, revenue planner, and reporting capabilities, so I could see my profitability, different revenue streams, and how much I was spending. This template is called the Be Your Own Boss template, and it's available for sale at www.breakyour budget.com/shop.

When first starting out, using a spreadsheet is the way to go. This is because it is far less overwhelming than the majority of bookkeeping software that exists, it's fully customizable, and it's manageable for you to set up and maintain entirely on your own.

Once you cross the six-figure mark in your business revenue or start hiring people, it's time to graduate to a bookkeeping software such as QuickBooks or Xero. These tools are definitely a bit more complicated to set up, but they can connect to all of your various bank accounts, credit cards, and payment systems to make the entire process a breeze. Plus, you can set up rules for recurring transactions and complete your bookkeeping in just a few minutes per week.

Given they can be a major challenge to get up and running correctly, I highly recommend hiring a professional to ensure that you are set up legally. Bookkeeping is *not* something you want to mess up, because it can result in misreporting your income and misfiling your taxes, which is a big no-no. If you are not confident in your ability to maintain your books on your own, hiring a bookkeeper is one of those business expenses that is definitely worth it.

Taxes

Small business and side hustle taxes are the bane of my existence. Even during the years where I kept immaculate books, there was always *something* tax-related that popped up to add additional stress to my life. If you are making money outside of a W-2 job, you need to take your taxes seriously.

When you make money through your business, the revenue you earn is not taxed before it clears your business bank account. That means that you need to set money aside each month to ensure when you do file your taxes, you have enough funds available to pay them. Generally speaking, this can be estimated around 30%–35% of your revenue, but different factors can impact this figure, from your expenses to the state you run your business in. Make sure you talk to an accountant to get specific guidance on your situation!

There are three steps to follow when creating a business finance system to pay your taxes:

Step 1: Maintain your books. You can do this by tracking your revenue and expenses regularly so you can see clear reporting on how much money you have made and spent throughout the tax year.

Step 2: Ensure you have your quarterly tax estimate deadlines clearly marked on your calendar. As a business owner, it's your responsibility to pay both your federal and state tax estimates on time. These fall in January, April, June, and September. Based on your projected revenue for the year, you are required to make quarterly tax payments. If you are not sure what your projected revenue will be, or how to project your revenue to help estimate your quarterly payments, you need to talk to an accountant. Are you catching a theme here? An accountant is a really important hire.

Step 3: Open a separate bank account to store your tax money. If you already have a business bank account, that's great. But if you keep the money you need for taxes in your business bank account where your cash flows in and out, it can be easy to lose track of how much you have and what it's meant for. I recommend opening up a high-yield savings account, call it your Business Tax Account, and at the end of each month when you are closing your books, transfer 30%–35% (or your accountant's recommendation) into your tax savings accounts.

By following this system, when the tax deadlines come around, you'll have the money set aside and ready to go, making a complicated process a lot easier.

Another quick tip to keep in mind that has caught me off guard in the past is related to your April estimated payments. Tax Day usually falls around April 15th for the previous tax year, meaning in April you may have to make two tax payments: your final payment for the prior tax year, if you owe money, *and* your Q1 estimate for the current tax year. If you aren't paying attention to your taxes and cash flow ahead of this, you may come up short on cash, which can result in late fees and penalties.

At the end of the day, taxes are annoying, but don't let them get in the way of running a successful business. Mark the important dates on your calendar, open a tax savings account, and set money aside each month to ensure you have enough. Once you get the hang of this process, it becomes a lot easier. Oh, and *hire an accountant!*

Profitability

There are hundreds of different ratios and metrics you can track related to your business revenue, expenses, and profit. But for a basic online, one-person business, there are a few key metrics that you should be keeping an eye on to both ensure your business is healthy and to make better business decisions.

First is your *net income*. This is how much money your business is taking home after accounting for all of your expenses and your taxes. When you hear someone refer to a "bottom line" in the context of business finances, they are referring to net income.

Next is *net profit margin,* which is your profitability after expenses and taxes. This is net income as a percentage of your revenue. The higher your profit margin, the more revenue your business is keeping. If you want to increase your net profit margin, look for ways to trim your expenses.

Beyond these two key measures of profitability, you'll benefit from paying attention to both how you are making and spending money within your business. This can help you predict trends, forecast revenue, and understand seasonality to help boost sales or buffer slower months.

Looking at your revenue, pay attention to your various revenue streams and the percentage each is making up of your total revenue on a monthly basis. Maybe you offer three different products or services, and you're finding that one product is driving 75% of your revenue every month. With this information, you can lean into scaling that product further, or shift your attention toward your other offers to help balance the ratio.

In another example, let's say you offer two products, and you find that one of them tends to have higher revenue during the winter months and the other during the summer months. With this information, you can better forecast your income and make business decisions based on the seasonality of the different products.

Understanding not only how much revenue you are making but where that revenue is coming from, what is driving it, and when you see peaks and valleys will make you a more agile business owner.

Beyond your revenue, the other key area to pay attention to are your expenses. Different businesses have different expenses, but it's likely you have some recurring monthly expenses, and then depending on your industry or offerings, you may have a few ad hoc expenses that come up. Look at how much you're spending every month and on what, and see if there are inefficiencies you can address to increase your profit margin. That could be switching from a monthly payment plan to an annual pay-in-full plan, or it could be canceling expenses for services or software you aren't using to their fullest extent.

Ultimately, as a business owner you own your numbers, and your business's financial health is directly related to your livelihood and quality of life. Knowing your numbers can help you optimize and scale your business, which in turn will help you create a stable source of income that you can rely on.

Business Finance System

How you manage your business finances is going to be up to you, but I do recommend implementing a weekly and monthly book-keeping routine into your workflow. I don't like to boil the ocean when it comes to this process, so here is how I manage my business finances. It is about 10 minutes per week, and 30 minutes at the end of the month.

Every Friday, I have a recurring 15-minute time slot on my calendar for my weekly bookkeeping. When the alarm goes off, I log into Xero, which is the accounting software that I use, and I categorize each of my revenue and expense transactions. I have tons of rules set up, so 90% of my transactions are pre-categorized, and I just need to hit OK.

For any nonrecurring transactions, or payments from brands, I like to add in additional details that will help my accountant. I will add in notes that identify which brand the payment is from or what a specific expense is related to. Detail can be extremely helpful when bookkeeping, so add it wherever you can.

Once I am done categorizing my transactions, I will usually take a few minutes to review my metrics. I like to look at my month-to-date revenue by type, as well as how much I've spent so far. This helps me maintain a regular pulse check on my business each week and minimizes the burden at the end of the month.

Once I reach the end of the month, I dedicate 30–60 minutes to close my books. Since I've already done the majority of my bookkeeping each week, during this time I am ensuring that all of my transactions have been properly categorized and accounted for, and I check my bank balances to ensure the balances reported in Xero match my bank account. This small check validates to me that everything is accurate; I learned this through working my various finance jobs.

Once I close my books at the end of the month, I like to take a deeper dive on my reporting. I'll look at the metrics I discussed earlier such as net profit margin, and I will pull my revenue numbers to see which products or deals drove the most business that month. I love analytics, so I dedicate time to this and will incorporate findings into my goals for the next month, quarter, and beyond.

Ultimately, this system is fairly low lift, but it keeps me in tune with my business finances. Bookkeeping is definitely not the most glamorous part of entrepreneurship, but it is arguably one of the most important things you can do to ensure your business stays afloat. When you think about it, if you don't have cash flow, you don't really have a business, do you?

Business finances can feel overwhelming, especially when you are planting the seeds to scale and ultimately jump into full-time entrepreneurship. My best advice is to take each element one step at a time. Focus on generating consistent, diverse, and recurring revenue. Then take time to scale and replace your income and set yourself up for long-term success.

When it comes to managing the money you are earning, find a system that works for you! At the beginning, this may feel challenging; let this excite you. Take the time to learn more about bookkeeping and business financial health, and as you get more comfortable you'll find it gets easier and easier to maintain.

Key Takeaways

- While there are drawbacks to self-employment such as unpredictability and an "always on" mentality, the pros far outweigh any cons. The ability to take full control of your life, increase your income, and lean into your passions make the challenges of self-employment worth it.
- One of the biggest mistakes an entrepreneur can make is leaving a full-time job too soon to go all in on a business. This is a bad idea, because it puts an enormous amount of pressure on the financial aspect of your business before it has the opportunity to mature.
- You are not ready to leave your full-time job until you have established two to three income streams with three months of recurring revenue, a business emergency fund, replaced your full-time income with your business revenue, and have determined a plan to replace your benefits such as health insurance and retirement savings.
- Business finances are very different from personal finances. When managing your business finances, you need to create a bookkeeping system along with a system to prepare and pay your quarterly and annual taxes. If you need help with this, hire an accountant!
- To manage your business finances, you need to implement a bookkeeping routine to stay on top of your revenue, expenses, and profit. I recommend a weekly routine to categorize your revenue and expenses in your bookkeeping system, as well as a monthly routine where you close your books, check your bank balances, and review your reports.

Chapter 9
You Are More Than Your Career

For the first half of my 20s, I equated my worth and my identity with my job title. If I wasn't doing the hardest job that made me sound like the smartest person in the room, I felt like a failure.

Because of this, I made my entire life revolve around work. I'd wake up at 5 a.m. to go to the gym or go on a run, and then I'd be showered, dressed, and fed with my butt in the chair at my desk at 8:30 a.m. Every day.

After work, I'd spend my evenings studying for my professional exams, attending some type of work event or happy hour, or preparing for the next day of work. I had very little social life during the week outside of my job, and at the time, I didn't realize how detrimental it was; I thought it was what everyone was doing.

On the weekends, I spent my Saturdays studying and my Sundays hanging out. I wasn't living; I was existing in a constant state of stress that I wasn't doing enough. There is enormous pressure on young professionals to do the most, and I was no exception. I held myself to a standard I could never meet, and it made me miserable.

I was consumed by my work in a bad way. I think a large part of this was because work provided a stability in my life that I no longer had. Up until you graduate college, your whole life is laid out for you. Once you enter the workforce, it's up to you to figure out *The Plan*. I wasn't happy with my social life or my living situation, so instead I poured myself into my job because it was something I could control. I didn't know what I wanted to do or who I wanted to be, and it was easier to forge ahead with the identity I created for myself at work than it was to explore those outside hobbies or lean into something that made me happy.

Crucial Career Takeaways

When the pandemic hit and our lives and schedules shifted overnight, I realized how exhausted and burnt out I was. I finally had time back in my day to sleep in and relax a bit more, and at first this made me antsy. I felt unproductive and stuck, which ultimately led to channeling that energy into Break Your Budget. It was through Break Your Budget that I began rewiring my perspective on work, slowly chipping away at the stronghold I had between my identity and my job title.

Leaning into my side hustle changed my life in more ways than one. In this final chapter, I want to leave you with some crucial career takeaways I wish I learned earlier. This section considers a few of the less-obvious impacts Break Your Budget has had on my career thus far.

My Job Is No Longer My Identity

I had an identity crisis when I quit my job. All of a sudden I went from "the girl who works in finance" to "the girl who quit her job to be an influencer." If I am being honest, one of the main reasons I stayed in my corporate job for so much longer than I financially needed to was because I was afraid of what life would be like without a job title to tell people. What would I say? What would they think?

These questions haunted me for months. What I told myself—and I still tell myself to this day—is that it doesn't matter what I do to pay my bills as long as my bills are paid. When I worked in finance, it implied to other people that I made good money. In a twisted way this made me feel confident, because it presented outwardly that I was successful. Being an "influencer" doesn't really give off the same vibe. The initial impression is usually something vain, or an assumption that I sit around all day and make videos or take pictures of myself.

Relinquishing my grasp on caring what other people think about my job has set me free. I have never felt more confident in my career decisions and myself than I do now. Running a business has forced me to step outside of my comfort zone, learn new skills, and put myself out there in ways I never would have done in my corporate job, and that's enough for me. If being happy means that someone out there may not respect my job title, I can live with that.

I Operate with Life-Work Balance

And yes, I mean life-work balance, not the other way around. I wasted years of my life working to live. I didn't prioritize anything else, and it led to a major identity crisis that has taken years to work through. Since I have been blessed with the ability to create my own schedule, I now prioritize living my life above work.

This doesn't mean that work isn't a priority or that I don't value my business, because I do. It's one of the most important pillars of my life. But that's all it is—*a pillar* of my life, not my whole life. I now prioritize my hobbies and interests, I make time for my social life during the week, and my weekends are for me, not for work. While there is always a struggle to create a hard boundary between work and life, I've found that giving myself the space to enjoy my life outside of work has made me significantly happier and more pleasant to be around.

I Am More Multifaceted Than I Knew

Because I equated my entire identity with my career in finance, I didn't value creative positions. I didn't think they were hard, or *as hard* as working in finance, and so I didn't give them much thought. What Break Your Budget has taught me is not only how challenging creative careers can be but how fun they can be, too!

I always thought work had to suck. It doesn't. In fact, my least favorite part of my job now is the finance stuff. I love the creativity—from creating videos to writing books to working with brands and everything in between. I'd almost argue that my passion has shifted away from finance and into creativity.

It's now July 2023 at the time of writing this book, and I look back on who I was in those early years of my 20s, and I don't recognize her. In fact, I can't even comprehend how I used to operate like that—it's no wonder I was so miserable and unhappy!

Embrace the Seasons of Your Career

While working on my own business and experiencing the joy that has been self-employment has helped me mend my toxic relationship with work, it's also made me realize how normal it is to move through seasons in your career. Your life will change, your priorities will change, and your interests will change; this is all normal in your 20s and beyond.

I hate how this ebb and flow isn't discussed and normalized. Instead, we are told that we constantly need to be grinding at work, climbing the ladder, vying for that next promotion or job-hopping to get the raise we deserve. It's ridiculous to think that we will operate this way for 45 years, and it can make working feel like a hopeless endeavor we can never truly escape from.

In my eyes, there are three main "seasons" of work, and they stem beyond simply learning and earning.

- **Advancement:** A season of advancement means you're willing to surrender to the grind. You're putting in the work to learn and earn to gain more experience to improve your finances.
- **Lifestyle balance:** This is a season where you still value your career, but you are more focused on exploring your goals outside

of work. This may include prioritizing family, leaning into hobbies, or simply taking the time to rest and recharge.

- **Transformation:** In this season you are ready to reinvent your career. You may be interested in switching jobs, changing career paths, starting a business, or taking that leap from side-hustle to full-time entrepreneurship.

At 28, I've already gone through all three of these seasons of work, and it's likely I will go through all three again multiple times over. Just like seasons throughout the year, it's natural for your priorities to shift. The season you are in will have a profound influence on the types of jobs you search for and the aspects that are important to you.

Prioritize Life-Work Balance

Beyond leaning into the idea of career seasonality, I want to emphasize the idea of life-work balance. Many companies use "work-life balance" as a selling point or benefit, but when you really think about it, this is absurd. Getting to live a balanced life as a "benefit" is a testament to how warped our perspective on work has become.

To achieve life-work balance and start prioritizing your time outside of work, which regardless of the season you are in is important, you need to implement some boundaries.

Here are a few boundaries to think about as we part ways.

Availability

Given the technology that exists today combined with the normalization of work from home, there is now an expectation that workers—both corporate and self-employed—are available 24/7.

When I worked my corporate job, I was on the clock from 8:30 a.m. to 5 p.m., but if someone needed me outside of those hours, there was an expectation for me to respond. Or if an "urgent" task came up later in the day, I had to work until it got done.

Now that I work for myself, the expectations around my working hours have shifted, and not necessarily in a better direction. If someone purchases a product from me and needs assistance, they expect a timely reply. If I am working with a brand and they need an adjusted piece of content, it needs to happen ASAP, even if I'm on vacation.

To alleviate the around-the-clock expectation, it's important to set clear boundaries around your availability. For me, this means working a regular nine-to-five schedule most of the time, and if I am taking time off, I put up an out of office so anyone who contacts me knows to expect a delay in my reply.

Action: Look at your schedule to determine your "available" hours, and then *communicate them* to the appropriate people.

Personal Priorities

Because work can be so overwhelming, it is increasingly difficult to prioritize self-care and personal time. To address this, add at least one personal priority to your daily to-do list. Whether it be a workout class, an errand, an extra 30 minutes with a family member, or anything in between, make sure you do something for yourself every day.

Action: Schedule personal time into your calendar, and keep the promise to yourself to stick to it!

Downtime

You need to fully take advantage of the time you do have away from work. Rather than spending your evenings passively checking your email or your weekends dwelling on what is waiting for you on Monday morning, make your time outside of your available hours a work-free zone.

When you step away from your desk or leave the office, your goal should be to mentally shift out of "work mode" and into "life mode."

Action: Remove your work email and applications from your phone so you are not tempted to check it in your free time.

Don't overlook the value of creating boundaries during every season of your career. Even if you are in a season of advancement, you still need to prioritize yourself, or else you'll end up like I did: burnt out and miserable as a result of your own expectations.

Final Thoughts

As I leave you with a handbook to navigate every corner of your career, I want to share some parting wisdom that I've gained in my short yet transformative experience working. I'm only 28, so I have about six years of work under my belt, but it feels like I've been working for an eternity.

First, don't seek happiness in your career from factors outside of your control. If you think finding a new job or getting a raise or changing managers is going to make your life better or make you feel more fulfilled, it won't. I hate to be the bearer of bad news, but the stimuli of starting a new job or making more money wears off pretty quickly. You'll realize these achievements don't fill the empty space you thought they would, and you'll be back spinning your wheels to reach the next one and end up in a perpetual cycle of nothingness.

Real happiness and satisfaction at work come from within. It sounds cliché, but your ability to turn inward and discover the aspects of work you enjoy will put you on the path to career fulfillment.

Second, make the conscious decision to live on your own terms, no matter what your job is or what anyone else thinks about it. Regardless of whether you work a corporate job or are self-employed, work is work. The minute you decide to turn your back on expectations from people around you—or the expectations you've placed on yourself—is when your life truly begins. I often look back at my own personal turning point and reflect on where I'd be if I hadn't decided to post the video or move to LA or quit my job when I felt disrespected.

No one else needs to understand your decisions because no one else has to live with them except for you.

And finally, you own your career. Not your manager, not your work bestie, not your partner or your parents. *You.* You are the one who is solely responsible for advocating for yourself, seizing opportunity, choosing to leave, or deciding that you deserve more.

Stop waiting for someone else's approval or permission to make the career moves that are going to catapult you to success. Stop looking to others for direction on what your next step is going to be. Stop letting the people around you scare you or judge you for deciding that you want more for yourself.

It's your life, your career, and your choice. Own it.

Appendix
Young Professional Career Profiles

O ne of the biggest challenges I see young professionals face is a lack of awareness or access to different job opportunities and career paths that exist. Throughout high school and into college, you're told that you need to pick a school, pick a major, and pursue a career path within that major. Deviating from this path is perceived as a setback.

The reality is that for many career paths, your major doesn't matter as much as you think it does. And once you enter the workforce, the experience and skill set you have hold far more weight than your college coursework or GPA.

As part of my goal to highlight various career paths and options that exist, I surveyed my social media audience and asked them questions about their career path, education background, and lessons learned through work.

On the following pages, I've condensed the information from 16 submissions. These are real people (I have withheld their names for privacy), with real jobs and real experience, who are also navigating their careers and seeking roles that provide personal, professional, and financial fulfillment.

They have all taken different paths; some conventional, some not. Some of them pursued a four-year degree; others went to trade school or community college. There are entrepreneurs, nurses, analysts, consultants; they are all on their own path, owning their careers, and leveraging their experience to find their own definition of success.

Profile #1

Age: 25

Location: Dallas, Texas

College/Major: Miami University, Architecture/Interior Design

Industry: Architecture

Job Title: Interior Designer and Medical Planner

Annual Salary: $60,000

Years of Experience: 2

Career Path Overview

I had many internships in college in the location I knew I eventually wanted to work, especially because I lived across the country from that city while I was an undergrad. I networked with many people to land at the firm I am with today, which I have been with for two years now.

What Do You Do at Work?

I am a health care interior designer and medical planner. I design mostly hospitals. My role on every project is to contribute and benefit the well-being of our health care systems and help hospitals become a more inviting and well-operated place to be. I help with the early stages of medical planning, which involves making sure the way we design it is a seamless operation for not only the doctors and nurses, but for patients and families who inhabit these spaces as well. Health care design has also become laser focused on sustainability and the goals of creating spaces in our environment that work toward that goal, such as carbon zero. This comes into play largely with the materials designers pick to inhabit these spaces, which is also part of my role. As many would assume, it would be counter-intuitive to design hospitals and places for sick patients loaded with finishes that give off chemicals that are bad for our health.

What Is Your Favorite Part of Your Job?

My favorite part of my job is knowing that our design choices make a huge difference and impact on patients, families, and doctors/nurses lives. Witnessing the continuously evolving and cutting-edge technology in our health care systems and designing for the future of health care as a country is extremely motivating as a designer of these spaces.

What Career Advice Would You Give to Your Younger Self?

My number one career tip would be network. Connections are the most valuable assets to have beyond your degree. Networking can open doors to new opportunities that might be out of reach otherwise. LinkedIn should be your best friend in college and as you're looking for jobs in the future.

Profile #2

Age: 27

Location: New York, New York

College/Major: Indiana University Bloomington, Advertising and Human-Centered Computing Design

Industry: Marketing

Job Title: Founder/CEO of a Product Design Agency

Annual Salary: $145,000–$195,000 (self-employed)

Years of Experience: 6

Career Path Overview

I put myself through college through freelance design work, part-time jobs, and utilized student loans to pay for school. After graduating I worked at two major tech companies, and now I'm focused on start-ups. I've been through over five reorganizations, and I have been through two layoffs. I'm now back working independently (which I never stopped) and formalized my business legally two years ago.

What Do You Do at Work?

I design digital experiences, including websites and mobile and desktop applications. I also design brand creative work and advise companies on how to build out creative operations for their business. Sometimes I help manage advertising campaigns as well.

What Is Your Favorite Part of Your Job?

While it can be lonely, building my own business is a creative project all in itself. I'm excited by meeting new people and learning how brands and companies are built. The ability to make my creative ideas tangible is something I don't take for granted.

What Career Advice Would You Give to Your Younger Self?

Write your narrative, or someone else will write it for you. The highest-performing people ask great questions.

Profile #3

Age: 30

Location: Los Angeles, California

College/Major: University of Delaware, Accounting and Finance

Industry: Accounting

Job Title: Senior Accounting Manager

Annual Salary: $126,000

Years of Experience: 8

Career Path Overview

I graduated college and went to work for a midsized public accounting firm in NYC. After two busy seasons I moved to LA and got into private accounting for start-ups. I worked as the only accountant at a 15-person custom packaging start-up. I then worked at an accounting consulting firm for three years before moving to a tech start-up to work in royalty accounting. Now I am back at one of my clients from the consulting firm.

What Do You Do at Work?

I am the only in-house accountant at a 90-person B2B SaaS company. I pay the bills, invoice customers, assemble monthly financial packages for the C-suite and board of directors, and I manage yearly external audits (done by a public accounting firm). I also do things like run payroll, process expense reimbursements, calculate and process sales commissions, and manage the company 401(k) benefits.

What Is Your Favorite Part of Your Job?

I loved landing in start-ups, where I get to be a crucial part of the operations team! I never would have imagined I could be a one-woman show at a 90-person company when I graduated college.

What Career Advice Would You Give to Your Younger Self?

There are so many jobs out there that you don't know exist yet. You don't have to stay in the quintessential "role" based on your major. Get a job at a company that resonates with you, and learn from people in all different departments. In corporate America, I think it's the best way to find a career that is meaningful to you.

Profile #4

Age: 27

Location: Philadelphia, Pennsylvania

College/Major: Drexel University, Public Health and Sociology

Industry: Health Care

Job Title: Infection Control Practitioner

Annual Salary: $91,000

Years of Experience: 4

Career Path Overview

I started my career at a restaurant where I worked as a host during college and post-grad. A few months after graduating I secured a position in my field, public health, at my city's public health department as a disease intervention specialist. I focused on STD transmission reduction and patient education, mainly for syphilis and HIV. Another aspect of my role there was working with the city prison department. Each week I visited the prisons to confirm treatment information and provide partner services. I worked at the health department for about two years.

Through working with the prison infection preventionist, I learned about the field of infection control, which is essentially public health for health care facilities. It encompasses epidemiology like my prior work did, but the focus is on reducing health care–associated infections.

From there I took an online course as a refresher in epidemiology, applied around, and eventually landed my current position at a hospital as an infection control practitioner. I have been there over two years and am currently studying for my Certification in Infection Control (CIC).

What Do You Do at Work?

I prevent and reduce health care–associated infections, including surgical site infections, catheter-associated urinary tract infections, and central line–associated bloodstream infections. I investigate outbreaks in health care settings and implement control measures to contain the outbreak. I work with inpatient and outpatient staff to ensure regulatory compliance and prepare them for Joint Commission and Department of Health surveys.

What Is Your Favorite Part of Your Job?

My favorite part of my path is the flexibility I've had with myself, and the unwavering faith I've had in my abilities. I changed industries because I knew I needed more money and better growth opportunities than what the health department could offer.

What Career Advice Would You Give to Your Younger Self?

Stay true to your mission, but don't be so tied to one path. You can stay aligned with your passion while looking for opportunities in other industries. Just because the stereotype is that public health is a low-paying field, and that a bachelor's in public health is useless, it doesn't mean that needs to be your reality.

Profile #5

Age: 24

Location: San Francisco, California

College/Major: University of Colorado Boulder, Sociology and Women/Gender Studies

Industry: Marketing and Technology

Job Title: Strategic Integration Marketing Manager

Annual Salary: $100,000

Years of Experience: 3

Career Path Overview

I transferred to CU in 2018 from fashion school to study sociology and minor in women and gender studies. I originally wanted to transfer into the communications school to study media/communications in fashion but was rejected because I transferred as a sophomore and not a junior. This credit limitation was disappointing, but I knew I still wanted to pursue media and communications and still could with my new major; my path would just look different.

I officially started my career in 2021, working as a freelance social media manager and content creator at a major beauty brand. This experience set the path for the rest of my career—to this day, I produce content on a freelance basis for this company and work in conjunction with their social media and influencer marketing teams.

By 2022, I was able to secure a position with one of the biggest technology companies in the world. During my time in tech we created a new space for their brand awareness marketing efforts. I started as an influencer marketing specialist, focusing on "community" and quickly evolved the role into an Instagram, YouTube, and TikTok Lead focusing cross functionally on promoting influencer efforts in short-form video content.

What Do You Do at Work?

The technology company I work for has almost 30 lines of business. We are a global company that has countless marketing efforts across all the lines of business. My job is to connect the dots, get everyone on the same page, and help all these marketing teams send one cohesive message.

What Is Your Favorite Part of Your Job?

My favorite part about my job is the company that I work for. It prioritizes its people above anything else, and I can see that through how they practice treating their people on a daily basis.

What Career Advice Would You Give to Your Younger Self?

You deserve to take up space and have a seat at the table. You have been given these opportunities for a reason, and you know more than you think; your age and limited experience is an advantage and not a limitation because it gives you a different perspective that carries value.

Profile #6

Age: 30

Location: Austin, Texas

College/Major: Arizona State University, Global Health

Industry: Health Care

Job Title: Staff Scientist

Annual Salary: $165,000

Years of Experience: 8

Career Path Overview

I couldn't afford my tuition after a scholarship ran out, so I began working full-time my junior year as a research assistant at a family doctor's office that had clinical research studies. I took night classes at the community college and online courses for upper division credits. I wanted to be an epidemiologist at the CDC (Centers for Disease Control) and kept sticking out the promotions in clinical research to gain more tangible skills. Eventually I realized I was having more impact on health outcomes in my current role than I would in a government job and found that my current position became more closely aligned with my values.

What Do You Do at Work?

I design clinical research studies for medications and medical devices that need to be proven as safe and effective before physicians can use them to treat patients. It is highly cross functional working with animal models, market needs, FDA and international equivalent competent authorities, public policy, biostatistics, and medicine.

What Is Your Favorite Part of Your Job?

Working with people all over the world to create strategic solutions that impact the health and lives of others.

What Career Advice Would You Give to Your Younger Self?

Your college GPA doesn't define you. Keep taking risks, and don't put so much pressure on yourself to have it all figured out—it will all unfold how it is meant to.

Profile #7

Age: 24

Location: Harrisburg, Pennsylvania

College/Major: Attended trade school to focus on Cosmetology

Industry: Cosmetology

Job Title: Nail Technician

Annual Salary: $80,000 (including tips)

Years of Experience: 7

Career Path Overview

I decided to try out a trade school while I was in my junior year of high school. I hated school and really just wanted to get out of the typical classroom. I was accepted into a cosmetology program at 16, and then I got my first assistant job at a salon and worked after school and on weekends.

What Do You Do at Work?

I am a licensed cosmetologist (hair, skin, nails), but chose to become a full-time nail technician specializing in manicures, liquid hard gel, and pedicures.

What Is Your Favorite Part of Your Job?

My favorite part of my career is working with my clients who I end up building strong relationships and connections with. At the specific salon I work at, we are in full control of our schedules. I can work or take off whenever I need to. Having a flexible work schedule makes me feel very in control of my time. Also, it makes me want to push myself to work and achieve new goals because we are 100 percent commission based.

What Career Advice Would You Give to Your Younger Self?

In my line of work, it is very easy to get walked over by demanding clients. It is important to set strict boundaries, like limiting coming in on days off to accommodate clients and trying not to get caught up in the problems your clients have in their lives. Some clients will treat beauty appointments as therapy sessions and expect you to listen, give advice, and have sympathy. It can be emotionally exhausting. But once you understand that, work can be very enjoyable!

Profile #8

Age: 29

Location: Boynton Beach, Florida

College/Major: Florida Atlantic University, Finance and Business Law

Industry: Real Estate/Law

Job Title: Commercial Real Estate Paralegal

Annual Salary: $81,500

Years of Experience: 10

Career Path Overview

I started working at a law firm as an administrative assistant while in college. In the summer of 2017, I was promoted to a paralegal. In the summer of 2018, after graduating, I went to work for my current company as a commercial real estate paralegal in their real estate department focused on telecommunications.

Originally my plan was to go into finance. I worked at the law firm while in college with no intentions of pursuing a legal career. I just needed a job, and the law firm was flexible, so I took it. I never thought I would continue my career in the legal field, but I've enjoyed it. I also get to put my finance degree to use occasionally when dealing with financial models and proration statements. At some point in the future, I want to be able to put my finance degree to good use. I enjoy numbers, spreadsheets, budgeting, and so on. I'm still exploring my options while enjoying my current season of career.

What Do You Do at Work?

In short, our department's main goal is to secure the ground interest underneath cell towers through a ground lease or a term/perpetual easement, which in turn makes a particular cell tower more appealing to carriers like AT&T or T-Mobile. Long form, I draft contracts, review title commitments and surveys, prepare closing documents, close real estate transactions, handle document recordings, and issue title policies.

What Is Your Favorite Part of Your Job?

The people I meet and the positive financial impact I provide to them. I deal with people all over the world. During the pandemic when a lot of people were being laid off, they turned to a ground lease buyout for an income. A ground lease buyout is when we buy out the lease's rental stream and in turn provide a lump sum payment for an easement. In addition, I contribute to keeping the world connected!

What Career Advice Would You Give to Your Younger Self?

Learn as much as you can from anyone. Take constructive criticism; it only helps you in the future. Befriend the elders in your industry, as they have a wealth of knowledge you can learn from.

Profile #9

Age: 28

Location: Summerville, South Carolina

College/Major: Miller-Motte Technical College, Surgical Technology (trade program, Associates degree)

Industry: Health Care, Accounting

Job Title: Project Coordinator for Invoicing and Permitting

Annual Salary: $65,000

Years of Experience: 2

Career Path Overview

I first started in health care with my surgical technology degree. Instead of working as a surgical technologist, I worked as a sterile processing technician, which is a lateral job. I worked in that role/field for almost four years. During the pandemic I changed fields and careers to commercial construction as an assistant project manager and assistant bookkeeper. I did that for three months before I was let go due to the pandemic.

I then pursued my passions in the equestrian industry and managed a barn for an established trainer. That was for a year and half before being recommended for a job with a custom home builder in residential construction. I accepted a job with the custom home builder in 2021 and have been there since with an ever developing role and scope of work.

What Do You Do at Work?

I manage the coding of all invoices received for every home we build and coordinate with our accountant what is completed and ready to be paid. I manage each home's budget to ensure that we are not going over budget and managing our profit margin per job. I submit all required documents to receive building permits that allow us to build these homes in their respective municipalities. I also take an active role in developing and implementing SOPs (standard operating procedures) to better improve the company's performance in all areas.

What Is Your Favorite Part of Your Job?

My favorite part is the budget management and the systems and processes management.

What Career Advice Would You Give to Your Younger Self?

Getting a degree can be helpful depending on the field of work, but if it feels limiting to pursue a small specific degree, then your career will likely be limiting as well. Pursue what interests you, and find or make the financial opportunities to sustain you.

Profile #10

Age: 29

Location: Los Angeles, California

College/Major: California State University Los Angeles, Criminal Justice

Industry: Real Estate

Job Title: Assistant Property Manager

Annual Salary: $64,000

Years of Experience: 5

Career Path Overview

I originally planned on going straight into law enforcement with a goal of becoming a homicide detective and retiring as one. However, during my final semester, I just felt like that career path wasn't for me. I still graduated because I didn't want to throw away the last four years of my life. I lived in LA for about two years and struggled to pinpoint a career I was interested in. I worked predominantly in restaurants as a host/server and loved the fast money but just was not fulfilled in life. I ended up moving back home and asking my older cousin to help me land a job with her company, which was in property management. I landed the role as a leasing consultant and absolutely loved it.

What Do You Do at Work?

As the assistant property manager, my role entails collecting rent, processing move outs by refunding security deposits, and processing move-in applications. By collecting rent I have to ensure that 98% of rent is collected each month before we close our financial books for the month. If rent is not paid by then, I have to file an eviction on the resident who has not paid. When processing refunds I collect cleaning invoices from our vendors and charge the cleaning fee to the resident. I check to see if the resident has paid their final month's rent and utilities and send a final invoice, which will either have a bill or a refund check. Outside of the administrative tasks, I am the point of contact for all resident inquiries, which includes resident complaints.

What Is Your Favorite Part of Your Job?

My favorite part of my job is that there is always something new every day, and this keeps the job exciting.

What Career Advice Would You Give to Your Younger Self?

Invest more time in several hobbies and career paths. Don't limit yourself career-wise.

Profile #11

Age: 26

Location: Newport Beach, California

College/Major: Chapman University, Accounting and Business Administration

Industry: Advisory

Job Title: Senior Consultant (Big Four)

Annual Salary: $122,000

Years of Experience: 4

Career Path Overview

I completed two internships with my current company during college, which then led to a full-time advisory internship. I started at the company after graduating college as a consultant in August 2019, was promoted to senior in June 2021, and am up for manager promotion by Summer 2024.

What Do You Do at Work?

I help large (mostly publicly traded) companies modernize and optimize their finance and accounting operations through process improvement, standardization, and technology implementations. My practice works on a vast array of projects within the finance and accounting space, but the work often entails conducting current state assessments, providing recommendations on how to standardize and improve processes, implementing technology solutions to help automate processes, documenting our findings, and tracking and reporting on project updates and status.

What Is Your Favorite Part of Your Job?

My favorite part is getting to see the issues that major companies face and helping alleviate pain points. I also enjoy getting to work with smart individuals from various backgrounds.

What Career Advice Would You Give to Your Younger Self?

You're not expected to know how to do everything. Even if it doesn't feel like it now, you are learning skills that will be useful as you progress in your career.

Profile #12

Age: 26

Location: Savannah, Georgia

College/Major: Western Michigan University, Aerospace Engineering

Industry: Airplane Manufacturing

Job Title: Flight Test Engineer

Annual Salary: $101,000

Years of Experience: 3

Career Path Overview

This is my first role out of college, and although I had previous internship experience, it was not in the flight test field. It was always a goal of mine to be in the flight test industry, and I am forever grateful that things aligned the way they did.

What Do You Do at Work?

To ensure an airplane is safe to be flown and produced, it needs to be able to perform certain maneuvers and general characteristics in air. Based on regulations developed by the FAA, I write test plans, execute testing in-flight and on-ground with test pilots, monitor and analyze data in-flight, further reduce and analyze data post-flight, and write an extensive report.

What Is Your Favorite Part of Your Job?

Definitely the flying and data analysis, because it allows me to see the airplane behavior, potentially establish the limitations and boundaries, and develop the safest and most reliable airplanes.

What Career Advice Would You Give to Your Younger Self?

Do the right thing. Do everything to the best of your ability. And do what you can to leave something better for the world.

Profile #13

Age: 35

Location: Santa Fe, New Mexico

College/Major: Lane Community College, Dental Hygiene

Industry: Dentistry

Job Title: Dental Hygienist

Annual Salary: Hourly, $52 per hour, average of 30 hours per week

Years of Experience: 12

Career Path Overview

I started at $40/hour right out of dental hygiene school. I spent three years working in pediatric dentistry. Now I'm at a general dental practice at $52/hour.

What Do You Do at Work?

I take X-rays, clean teeth, provide oral cancer screenings, treat gum disease, provide oral hygiene instruction, present treatment plans, and schedule appointments.

What Is Your Favorite Part of Your Job?

Getting to know my patients and helping them make improvements in their health. I only work four days per week.

What Career Advice Would You Give to Your Younger Self?

Practice proper ergonomics from day one and stay active. Dental hygiene takes a toll on your body and you need to stay ahead of it.

Profile #14

Age: 31

Location: Billings, Montana

College/Major: Montana State University, Accounting and Finance

Industry: Accounting

Job Title: Credit Analyst

Annual Salary: $83,000

Years of Experience: 7

Career Path Overview

Right before graduating college I realized I didn't want to get my CPA (Certified Public Accountant), so I took an internship in a project management department to get my feet wet in the corporate world. After a few years, I came across a credit analyst position at a bank and thought it would be something I enjoyed that also played into my skill sets developed in college. I've come to realize just because you get an accounting degree, doesn't mean you have to do taxes or be a CPA!

What Do You Do at Work?

Perform credit/financial analysis for business banking customers to determine credit worthiness and credit rating. Prepare credit presentations/reports to make lending decisions on new and existing banking customers. Evaluate customer portfolios to maximize customer banking experience and minimize risk and potential loss to the bank.

What Is Your Favorite Part of Your Job?

My favorite part about my job is the puzzle of analyzing a customer's financials and portfolio to identify what's going on with the borrower and where I can boost their strengths and help with weaknesses. I enjoy problem-solving and analyzing a business's financials.

What Career Advice Would You Give to Your Younger Self?

Before I started my career I wish I would have told myself to write down my strengths and things I wanted out of a job. You don't have to take the conventional career path based on your major. Find a career path that plays on things you enjoy and your strengths; it's still a job, but you'll enjoy it more that way.

Profile #15

Age: 27

Location: Waterbury, Vermont

College/Major: University of Vermont, Nursing

Industry: Health Care

Job Title: Travel Operating Room Registered Nurse (RN)

Annual Salary: $100,000–$150,000 depending on accepted contracts

Years of Experience: 5

Career Path Overview

I started as a new graduate nurse in the operating room and then went to Nashville to do a paid internship where I gained general operating room experience. I moved back closer to home during the pandemic and got an operating room job in Boston. In 2022, I decided to quit and start travel-nursing. I spent most of that year up in Burlington, Vermont, (where I went to college) as a traveler. I was able to travel and take time off in 2023 and spent time in Salt Lake City. I nannied and skied for the winter. When I came back home I took a travel assignment at Dartmouth, where I am currently working in their vascular operating room. The operating room is intense and requires a lot of mental energy, but it has been a great way for me to earn money with my degree. Travel-nursing has given me financial freedom. I have been able to pay off my car and student loans, while also investing.

What Do You Do at Work?

An operating room nurse is someone who is there with you during a surgical operation. They assist with anesthesia and with surgeons to provide optimal surgical outcomes. The OR nurse is responsible for the patient when they are under anesthesia, helping place additional lines (IVs, Foley, and so on), and prepping the patient and room for surgery. We are also responsible for sterile instruments and sterile fields. There are two nurses (or a nurse and a scrub tech) for every case. We always have one patient to care for at a time. The OR is unique in that we work very closely with attending surgeons on a daily basis. We make sure to know their surgical preferences as well as their anticipated needs for the cases they have scheduled in a 12-hour shift.

What Is Your Favorite Part of Your Job?

My favorite thing about my job is learning directly from the physicians. I get to be a part of incredible surgeries that can be life-changing for the patients.

What Career Advice Would You Give to Your Younger Self?

Nursing can be extremely discouraging. Keep looking for an area of nursing that works for you that you find interesting. Everyone is burnt out, and it is hard to find a work-life balance.

Profile #16

Age: 27

Location: Denver, Colorado

College/Major: Florida Southern College, Biology, and Spanish. MBA Supply Chain Management and Health Care Management

Industry: Construction

Job Title: Management Trainee Program, Assistant Branch Manager

Annual Salary: $102,000

Years of Experience: 2

Career Path Overview

While in college, I worked in retail and the Student Admissions Building while also volunteering at a nonprofit clinic. I learned a lot of skills on how to be organized, think outside the box, analyze data, and how to speak with customers/clients. Toward the end of my bachelor's, I honestly did not know what I wanted to do, and was presented the opportunity to get my MBA. I knew this degree would provide me the skills and perspective to leverage ideas and knowledge I learned from my science classes into actionable skills and concepts in any work setting. I was then recruited to my current job. Honestly, I didn't think I would stay long, but the pandemic and fear convinced me to take the job and take a chance on the position, and I am glad I did. The skills and projects I have worked on will make me a great candidate for wherever I plan on going to. Plus, I am making pretty great money just two years out of my master's. I know I can make more elsewhere soon, so I will be working on my resumé and touching up my LinkedIn for when I am ready to start looking again.

What Do You Do at Work?

Business operations and sales enablement. Each ABM's (assistant branch manager) role in their branch is slightly different. At my location, I focus on moving obsolete and expired material, work with the supply chain team and pricing team on discrepancies on invoices to maximize profit potential, do inventory control with daily cycle counts, receive material, help manage our fleet by scheduling and routing delivery trucks, and also work on any special or large projects for customer material orders. At the end of the day, I'm "the fixer." If something needs to be looked into, dug into, and so on, I'm the person to lead the charge.

What Is Your Favorite Part of Your Job?

My favorite part has been the flexibility my manager has given me. While I do have daily tasks, I am able to work on any set of problems I choose to do and am trusted to get it done. My results are evident, as our location is now profitable and running smoothly.

What Career Advice Would You Give to Your Younger Self?

1. Your degree doesn't matter; the knowledge and the skills you get from it do!
2. Always be willing to seek out opportunities; you never know what you like until you try!
3. Negotiate, negotiate, negotiate.

References

Allocca, M. 2023. *Own Your Own Money*. Fair Winds Press.

BLS. 2023a. "Economic News Release: Table A-1. Employment Status of the Civilian Population by Sex and Age." US Bureau of Labor Statistics. https://www.bls.gov/news.release/empsit.t01.htm.

BLS. 2023b. "Occupational Employment and Wage Statistics: Occupational Employment and Wages, May 2022, 11-1011 Chief Executives." US Bureau of Labor Statistics. https://www.bls.gov/oes/current/oes111011.htm#(1).

Cultivated Culture. 2021. "Resume Statistics: We Analyzed 125,000+ Resumes, Here's What We Learned." https://cultivatedculture.com/resume-statistics/.

Ladders. 2018. "Eye-Tracking Study." https://www.theladders.com/static/images/basicSite/pdfs/TheLadders-EyeTracking-StudyC2.pdf.

Murphy, B. 2019. "Google Recruiters Say Using the X-Y-Z Formula on Your Resume Will Improve Your Odds of Getting Hired at Google." *Inc.* https://www.inc.com/bill-murphy-jr/google-recruiters-say-these-5-resume-tips-including-x-y-z-formula-will-improve-your-odds-of-getting-hired-at-google.html.

Newport, C. 2016. *Deep Work: Rules for Focused Success in a Distracted World*. Grand Central Publishing.

ResumeGo. n.d. "Resume Study: How LinkedIn affects the Interview Chances of Job Applicants." https://www.resumego.net/research/linkedin-interview-chances/.

About the Author

Michela Allocca created Break Your Budget in 2019 as a side hustle while working a full-time corporate job in the finance industry. Like many other young professionals, she struggled to find satisfaction at work while navigating all of the big life changes that happen during those pivotal post-grad years. Recognizing that she wasn't alone in this feeling, Michela turned to Break Your Budget as an outlet to share her journey making professional and financial decisions in her 20s. Now, she shares her story and lessons learned with the masses through educational content that speaks directly to the growing number of young people who are ready to take their professional power back.

Michela was born and raised in Boston, Massachusetts, and earned her bachelor's degree in finance from Elon University. She spent five years working a corporate job in various positions within the financial industry before scaling Break Your Budget to a seven-figure business with over one million followers across social media platforms. In 2023, Michela published her debut book, *Own Your Money*, where she shares practical strategies to navigate your finances in your 20s and beyond. She currently resides in Los Angeles, where she operates Break Your Budget full-time and enjoys the wonderful lifestyle that Southern California has to offer.

Index